Monuments and Memorials of Washington, D.C.

Allan M. Heller

Schiffer Publishing Ltd®

4880 Lower Valley Road, Atglen, PA 19310 USA

Dedication

To Hilda M. Miller (1918-1989). I always promised that I would
write something for you. I'm sorry that it took me so long.

Front cover: Dante Alighieri and United States Marine Corps photos by Maureen R.
Quinn. John Marshall photo by Franz Jantzen; collection of the Supreme Court of the
United States.

Designed by Mark David Bowyer
Type set in Bernhard Modern BT / Humanist 521 BT

ISBN: 0-7643-2418-7
Printed in China

Published by Schiffer Publishing Ltd.
4880 Lower Valley Road
Atglen, PA 19310
Phone: (610) 593-1777; Fax: (610) 593-2002
E-mail: Info@schifferbooks.com

For the largest selection of fine reference books on this and related subjects, please
visit our web site at **www.schifferbooks.com**
We are always looking for people to write books on new and related subjects. If you
have an idea for a book please contact us at the above address.

This book may be purchased from the publisher.
Include $3.95 for shipping.
Please try your bookstore first.
You may write for a free catalog.

In Europe, Schiffer books are distributed by
Bushwood Books
6 Marksbury Ave.
Kew Gardens
Surrey TW9 4JF England
Phone: 44 (0) 20 8392-8585; Fax: 44 (0) 20 8392-9876
E-mail: info@bushwoodbooks.co.uk
Website: www.bushwoodbooks.co.uk
Free postage in the U.K., Europe; air mail at cost.

Contents

Acknowledgments 5

Introduction 7

1. From Capitol Hill to Union Station 11
    Authority of Law and
        Contemplation of Justice 11
    Christopher Columbus
        Memorial Fountain 13
    James A. Garfield 16
    James Madison 18
    Nathanael Greene 18
    Peace Monument 20
    Robert A. Taft 22
    Ulysses S. Grant 23
    Veterans of Foreign Wars
        Memorial 25
    Winged Statue of Freedom atop
        the Capitol Dome 27

2. From the National Mall to
        Chinatown 31
    Albert Pike 31
    Andrew Jackson Downing
        Memorial Urn 33
    Andrew W. Mellon Memorial
        Fountain 33

Benjamin Banneker Fountain 34
Benjamin Franklin 35
Casimir Pulaski 37
The Future and The Past 38
George Gordon Meade 40
Grand Army of the Republic
    Monument 41
Heritage and Guardianship 43
John Marshall 45
Joseph Henry 46
Lincoln Statue 47
Louis Daguerre 48
Nathan Hale 49
National Law Enforcement
    Officers Memorial 50
U.S. Navy Memorial 53
William Blackstone 57
Winfield Scott Hancock 57

3. From the Washington
        Monument West 61

3a. Lafayette Park, the White
        House, & the Ellipse 61
    Albert Gallatin 62

Alexander Hamilton 64
Andrew Jackson 65
Boy Scout Memorial 68
David G. Farragut 69
First Division Monument 71
Friedrich Wilhelm von Steuben 73
Gilbert de Lafayette 75
James B. McPherson 77
Jean de Rochambeau 77
John Barry 79
John J. Pershing/American
    Expeditionary Forces
    (AFF) Memorial 80
Second Division Memorial 82
Settlers of the District of
    Columbia Memorial 83
Thaddeus Kosciuszko 83
William Tecumseh Sherman 85

3b. From the White House
        to the Kennedy Center 89
    Albert Einstein 89
    Alexander Pushkin 91
    Armenian Earthquake
        Memorial (Motherland) 92

Benito Juarez 94
Founders of the DAR
     (Daughters of the
     American Revolution)
     Memorial 94
Jane A. Delano Memorial/
     The Spirit of Nursing 96
John A. Rawlins 98
José Artigas 99
Korean War Veterans Memorial 100
Queen Isabella I 103
Red Cross Monument
     (Red Cross Spirit) 105
Signers of the Declaration of
     Independence Monument 108
Simon Bolivar 109
Vietnam Veterans Memorial 110
Vietnam Women's Memorial 114

3c. From the Washington
     Monument to the Lincoln
     Memorial 117
John Paul Jones 117
Lincoln Memorial 119
Washington Monument 121
World War I Memorial 124
World War II Memorial 125

3d. The Tidal Basin 129
     Cuban American Friendship
     Urn/U.S.S. Maine Memorial 129

Franklin Delano
     Roosevelt Memorial 130
George Mason National
     Memorial 137
Jefferson Memorial 139

3e. Crossing the Potomac,
     National Cemetery
     and the Environs 145
Iwo Jima/United States
     Marine Corps Memorial 145
John Ericsson 147
John F. Kennedy/The Eternal
     Flame 148
Lyndon Baines Johnson 151
Navy-Marine Memorial 151
Theodore Roosevelt 154
Tomb of the Unknowns 158

4. Further Afield 163
     Adams Memorial 163
     African American Civil War
          Memorial 165
     Daniel Webster 168
     Dante Alighieri 171
     Edmund Burke 172
     Emancipation Monument 173
     George B. McClellan 175
     George H. Thomas 176
Henry Wadsworth
     Longfellow 177

James Buchanan 178
Joan of Arc 181
John A. Logan 183
John Carroll 184
John Witherspoon 186
Lieutenant General George
     Washington 188
Mahatma Gandhi 191
Martin Luther 194
Mary McLeod Bethune 196
Nuns of the Battlefield 198
Philip H. Sheridan 199
Robert Emmet 201
Samuel Francis Dupont
     Memorial Fountain 203
Samuel Gompers 204
Samuel Hahnemann 206
Taras Shevchenko 209
Thomas Hopkins Gallaudet 209
Titanic Memorial 211
Winfield Scott 212

Bibliography 214

Index 222

Acknowledgments

I wish to thank the following individuals, without whose assistance this book could never have been completed:

Maureen R. Quinn and Janet L. Greentree, of the Bull Run Civil War Round Table; Bruce R. Mendelsohn, Communications Director for the National Law Enforcement Officers Memorial Fund; Brian Sharpe, of Sons of Confederate Veterans; Haik Gugarats, of the Armenian Embassy; Heather K. Calloway, of The Supreme Council, 33°, of the Ancient and Accepted Scottish Rite of Free-Masonry; Janice F. Goldblum, archivist for the National Academy of Sciences; Susan Raposa, Technical Information Specialist for the Commission of Fine Arts; Col. Cindy Gurney, Vietnam Women's Memorial Foundation, Inc.; Jean Waldman, Volunteer Nurse Historian, American Red Cross; Debbie Weixl, Public Relations, American Bar Association; Joe Davis, VFW Director of Public Affairs, Washington, D.C.; William Line, Communications Officer, National Capital Region, National Park Service; Joel Thoreson, Reference Archivist, Evangelical Lutheran Church in America; Heather Milke, editor of *By George!* (George Washington University); Professor Peter Rollberg, chair of German and Slavic languages and literature, George Washington University; Elizabeth E. McDonald, Communications Specialist, Georgetown University; Susan Robbins Watson, Archivist, American Red Cross; Ann E. Bartholomew, Registrar, American Red Cross Museum; Christy Batchelor and Roger Morgan, of the Boy Scouts of America National Council; Julie Woodford, University Relations Photographer, George Washington University; Robert M. Heller; David G. Goldstein; Todd Byrd, Office of Public Relations, Gallaudet University; Sandra M. Chase, MD, DHt; Jewel Anderson, of the Georgia Historical Society; Cynthia E. and David D. Jones; and finally, past and present members of Wordwrights (there, Jeffery)!

Map locating most of the statues and monuments discussed in this guide. *Map courtesy of the National Park Service, U.S. Department of the Interior.*

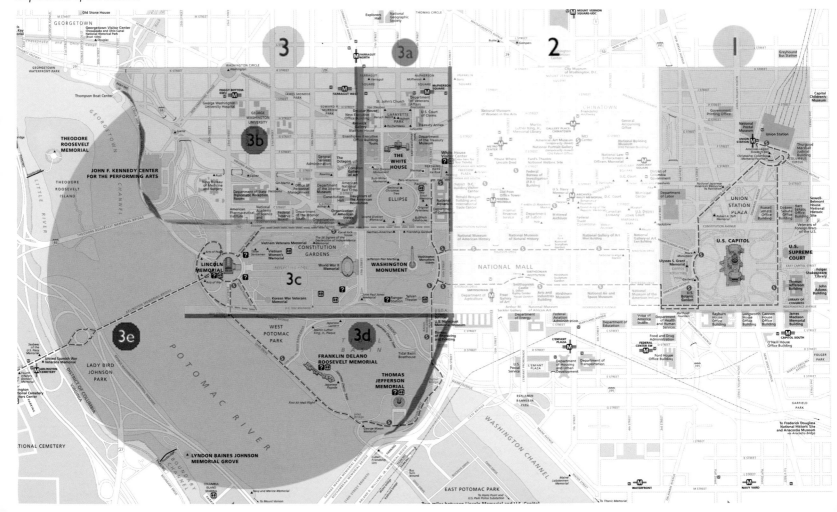

Introduction

The grave of Pierre Charles L'Enfant sits on a hill in Arlington National Cemetery, overlooking the city across the Potomac River that the French engineer helped design over 200 years ago. A young L'Enfant had arrived in America during the Revolutionary War, and had served in the Continental Army. He earned the respect of George Washington, and when the first president selected the site for Federal City in 1791, he appointed L'Enfant to lay out the plans. The ambitious Frenchman had lofty aspirations for the capital, and envisioned grand avenues radiating from central axes. Much of his inspiration he drew from Versailles, the seventeenth century palace built by French monarch Louis XIV, the "Sun King." Assisting L'Enfant in the designs was Major Andrew Ellicott.

Unfortunately for L'Enfant, his ambition proved his undoing. The headstrong Frenchman was stubborn and belligerent. When a private residence was in the path of one of L'Enfant's proposed avenues, he had the house demolished. President Washington was forced to take action. L'Enfant was informed that his services would no longer be required, and he was offered a compensatory stipend, which he refused. Ellicott was placed in charge of the project, and Benjamin Banneker, a free black and son of a former slave, was hired to help Ellicott with the surveying. In executing his plans, Ellicott remained mostly faithful to the ones originally drawn up by L'Enfant. The embittered L'Enfant died a broken, forgotten man in 1825, at the age of seventy.

Land for Federal City had been taken from the states of Virginia and Maryland, and formed a diamond-shaped, sixty-seven-square-mile tract whose central point was the confluence of the Potomac and Anacostia rivers, the latter known as the East Fork at the time. The area was officially designated the District of Columbia, to honor the fifteenth century Italian explorer credited with discovering the New World. Much of the land was barely habitable – a marshy, mosquito-infested wilderness. But most early cities had been founded along riverbanks, and Washington believed that the proximity of the waterways would be a tremendous benefit for commerce. In this he was ultimately mistaken; today, Washington, D.C.'s number one industry is not industry but government, seconded by tourism.

In 1800, the national capital was changed from Philadelphia to Federal City. The following year, the name became Washington, D.C., after the first president, who had died two years earlier. The ensuing decades saw the gradual removal of debris, and the reclamation of former swampland. Buildings sprouted where once quagmire and mud had held sway. Washington, D.C. became, in fact, a bona fide city.

Today, Washington is not merely the seat of government, but a repository of American culture and history, evidenced by myriad monuments erected to commemorate great men and women, significant events, magnificent triumphs, and searing tragedies. Memories molded in marble and bronze began filling up the district, so many that in 1986, the passage of the Commemorative Works Act stipulated that any future monuments or memorials in the capital would require an act of Congress.

Today, monuments and memorials dot the traffic circles in the city, they stand in state in the parks, and on the Mall. They guard the entrances of buildings to which they have some deep connection, and flank the façades of august institutions. Many are traditional bronze sculptures, poised upon lofty pedestals bearing identifying inscriptions. Others are peaceful and contemplative, centered on parks or fountains. The pomp and circumstance which attended most of the dedication ceremonies have long since faded, but these tangible testaments to the past remain. They remind us of our humanity, of the commonalties which bind us all. Perhaps, from behind the veil, L'Enfant somehow knows that he has made an indelible mark on the world, despite his ignominious departure. Perhaps he can at last rest in peace.

A.M.H., Philadelphia, Pennsylvania, July 15, 2005

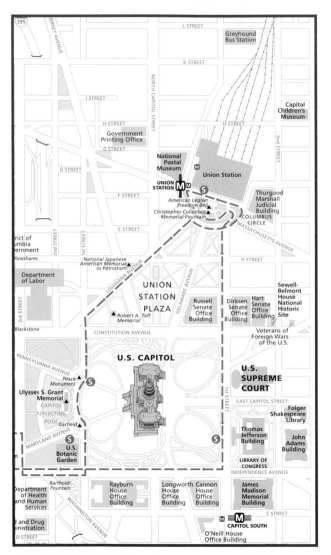

Map locating most of the statues and monuments discussed in this section of the guide. *Map courtesy of the National Park Service, U.S. Department of the Interior.*

1

From Capitol Hill to Union Station

Authority of Law and Contemplation of Justice

A prolific sculptor who created more than half a dozen works for the District alone, James Earle Fraser is best remembered for his 1913 design of the Buffalo nickel. Like any true artist, Fraser wanted to transcend mere aestheticism. He felt that his sculptures should not simply be harmonious with their surroundings, but also enhance the symbolism of the structures that they adorned. In executing his design for the pair of statues that flank the main steps of the Supreme Court, Fraser wrote to architect Cass Gilbert that the figures should symbolize the "grandeur and simplicity of the Supreme Court room" (U.S. Supreme Court). Fraser was a member of the Commission of Fine Arts from 1920 until 1925. Gilbert, an architect whose influence helped Fraser obtain the $90,000 commission, is represented by one of the figures in Robert Aitken's ornate bas-relief, "Equal Justice Under Law," which is carved on the pediment.

Sculpted by James Earle Fraser, the Authority of Law flanks the main steps of the Supreme Court. *Photo by Steve Petteway, collection of the Supreme Court of the United States.*

Sculpted by James Earle Fraser, the Contemplation of Justice flanks the main steps of the Supreme Court. *Photo by Steve Petteway, collection of the Supreme Court of the United States.*

Since 1935, the ten-foot white marble statues atop their fifty-ton blocks have anchored the steps of the court's west entrance. At right is the Authority of Law, a seated man dressed in a toga. Inscribed on the tablet that he holds in his left hand is the word "LEX" – Latin for "law." Behind the tablet is the sword by which the law is enforced. His demeanor is austere, but not at all menacing. Opposite him sits his female counterpart, the Contemplation of Justice. In her right hand she holds the blind-folded figure of Justice, while her left arm rests on a book of laws. Her expression is serene and thoughtful, appropriately "contemplative." Fraser took three years to complete the sculp-tures, which were installed shortly after the Supreme Court first opened.

Location: The Supreme Court, East Capitol and First Street.

Christopher Columbus Memorial Fountain

Rendered magnificently in marble by Lorado Taft, the fifteen-foot Christopher Columbus is peacefully oblivious to the conflict-ing historical evidence and changing political climate that have tar-nished his legacy. Draped regally in a long cloak, arms folded across his chest, he displays perhaps the faintest hint of arrogance in his chiseled stare. Even 513 years after his famous voyage, who would dare suggest to the Italian explorer that his likeness should be re-placed by one of Leif Erikson or Erik the Red? He stands boldly atop the prow of a ship, from which the figurehead of Discovery juts out. Behind Columbus, a globe encircled by four eagles rests atop a forty-five-foot granite shaft. On either side of the shaft, two marble men crouch diffidently on their haunches. A half-naked Indian brave to the right of Columbus represents America, and an old man opposite him, Europe.

In addition to being a hallmark of aesthetic achievement, the Columbus Memorial Fountain strikes viewers with its artis-tic symmetry. Anchoring the fountain's east and west ends are two reclining lions, the rectangular bases on which they rest reminiscent of Egyptian mastabas. Three flagpoles – represent-ing the *Nina*, *Pinta,* and *Santa Maria,* are spaced evenly behind the fountain. Atop each flagpole is a globe surmounted by a single eagle.

A panoramic view of the fountain is almost anachronistic: the stately, Doric colonnade of Union Station dominates the background with its massive arched entrances, and its row of stone Centurions perennially standing guard on a ledge above the pillars. And in front, a fifteenth-century sailor with his mot-ley, marble crew.

The Spanish rulers who financed Columbus's 1492 expedi-tion are relegated to relative obscurity in comparison with the piece's other elements. A three-foot diameter bas-relief me-dallion portrait on the rear, or south side, of the granite shaft depicts King Ferdinand and Queen Isabella.

In designing the memorial fountain, Daniel Burnham was inspired by a similar work by Frederick MacMonnies which was created for the World Fair in Chicago in 1893 (see George B. McClellan statue, p. 175). Burnham, a prominent Chicago architect, became the first chairman of The Commission of Fine Arts in 1910. Nine years prior to that, he had served on the newly-created Senate Park Commission, chaired by Michigan senator James McMillan.

The Columbus Memorial Fountain was erected by The Knights of Columbus in 1912, five years after Washington, D.C's Union Station opened.

Location: In front of Union Station, Massachusetts Avenue and First Street, N.E.

Lorado Taft's memorial fountain to Italian explorer Christopher Columbus has graced Union Station for nearly a century. *Photos by Janet L. Greentree.*

James A. Garfield

James A. Garfield's claim to immortality is ironically based on his untimely death, which made him the second president, after Abraham Lincoln, to be assassinated, and the fourth one to die in office. Only William Henry Harrison, who caught a fatal bought of pneumonia after giving a long inaugural address in frigid weather, served a shorter term – a little less than a month. After only four months as president, Garfield was shot in July of 1881 by Charles Guiteau, a disgruntled office seeker. Guiteau had supported Garfield's presidential campaign, but became vengeful after Garfield failed to fulfill a supposed promise to appoint Guiteau to a consular position. After the attack, Garfield lingered for two and a half months before expiring. Guiteau was executed the following year.

Like Ulysses S. Grant and Rutherford B. Hayes before him, Garfield was a former Civil War general, and his old comrades-in-arms promptly campaigned for a memorial. After a relatively short period of six years, the tribute was unveiled. The dedication was attended by President Grover Cleveland and his cabinet, along with hundreds of veterans and Garfield's fellow members of the Society of the Army of the Cumberland.

Measuring nine feet tall, Garfield stands with his left leg slightly extended, and with his left hand clutching a piece of paper to his chest. His right hand rests on a podium. Flanked by bronze bas relief panels, the inscription on the front of the round pedestal on which he stands reads: "JAMES A. GARFIELD/1831-1881."

The Society of the Army of the Cumberland raised this memorial to slain President James A. Garfield in 1887, six years after his assassination. *Photos by Janet L. Greentree.*

Three bronze sculptures seated on a ledge around the base of the monument show a counterclockwise chronology of the life of the twentieth president. To the lower right of the central figure, the musing scholar Garfield reads from a scroll. To the left is the bearded young soldier Garfield, one hand poised on the pommel of a sword. Opposite these two, not visible from the front of the monument, the middle-aged politician Garfield is seated by a pile of books. He is holding a tablet on which is written "Law-Justice-Prosperity." A bronze wreath encircles the pedestal, just above the heads of the three reclining figures and below the bas-relief panels. Original plans called for the three sculptures to be nude.

On one side of the base is the inscription "ERECTED/BY HIS COMRADES/OF THE/SOCIETY OF THE ARMY/OF THE/CUMBERLAND/MAY 12, 1887," while the inscription on the opposite side reads "MAJOR GENERAL U-S-V./MEMBER OF CONGRESS,/SENATOR,/AND/PRESIDENT/OF THE/UNITED STATES/OF/AMERICA." Behind the Garfield monument, the Capitol dome rises in the background, its Freedom sculpture an exclamation point against the Washington, D.C. sky.

The memorial was designed by architect Richard Morris Hunt, and sculpted by John Quincy Adams Ward (see George H. Thomas Memorial, p. 176). About half of the $55,000 cost was raised by the Society of the Army of the Cumberland, which held a memorial fair for that purpose. Congress kicked in the rest of the money.

Location: 1ˢᵗ Street and Maryland Avenue S.W.

James Madison

This marble sculpture of James Madison is appropriately placed in front of the Madison Building of the Library of Congress, an institution which he was instrumental in founding. Madison is seated casually with his right leg extended slightly, and holding a book in his right hand. The book in his hand is supposed to be volume eighty-three of the *Encylopédie Méthodique*. Even prior to his enrolling at the College of New Jersey – later Princeton University – Madison had learned French, Greek, and Latin.

Madison served as the fourth president of the United States, from 1809-1817. Of small stature and delicate health, he was often under tremendous strain during his presidency, particularly when war broke out with Great Britain over the seizure of American ships. Napoleon's rise to power also brought the possibility of war with former ally, France. But Andrew Jackson's routing of the British at New Orleans in 1815, followed by news of a peace treaty with England signed a month prior to that, vindicated Madison. Napoleon's defeat at Waterloo that same year nullified another threat to the burgeoning nation.

As a delegate from Virginia to the Continental Congress in 1787, Madison was at odds with Patrick Henry, a staunch anti-Federalist opposed to the Constitution. Madison was fortunate to have the support of Thomas Jefferson, with whom he maintained a lifelong friendship. Never one to take a passive role in politics, Madison co-authored *The Federalist Papers* with Alexander Hamilton and John Jay, and was instrumental in drafting the Bill of Rights (see George Mason National Memorial, p. 137). When he was forty-three, he married Dolly Payne Todd, a twenty-five-year-old widow with a young son. Madison died in 1836, at the age of eighty-five.

Location: Independence Avenue and 2nd Street, at the Madison Building of the Library of Congress.

Nathanael Greene

Major General Nathanael Greene (1742-1786) lived to see his country win her independence from Great Britain in 1783, but did not live much longer after that, dying at the age of forty-four at his farm in Savannah, Georgia. His greatest military effort was actually a defeat for his much larger American forces that clashed with English General Lord Charles Cornwallis, who himself was to surrender to George Washington later that year. The site of the March 15, 1781, battle, where Greene's men were eventually forced to withdraw after inflicting heavy losses on the enemy, is today the site of a national military park.

During the revolution, Greene commanded Rhode Island's militia, which he was instrumental in founding in 1774. In 1780, Washington placed him in charge of the Southern Department of the American Army. In this latter capacity he squared off against Cornwallis's British regulars and Hessian mercenaries at the aforementioned skirmish, which took place at Guilford Courthouse in Greensboro, North Carolina.

Many Americans have the misconception that the Continental forces regularly trounced the British troops, leaving the English no alternative but to abandon their colonial possessions. In fact, the overwhelming majority of battles resulted in British victories, but attrition and financial considerations eventually took their toll on the Crown. Throughout the southern campaign, Greene brilliantly played a cat-and-mouse game with Cornwallis, gradually wearing the British down by forcing them to engage in prolonged pursuits.

Congress appropriated $50,000 for the thirteen-foot bronze equestrian statue of Major General Nathanael Greene that stands at Maryland and Massachusetts avenues in Stanton Park. Dedicated in 1877, the sculpture features the general in full uniform, his sheathed saber hanging at his left flank. His right hand points straight ahead, while his left hand holds the reins. The oblong pedestal, about thirteen feet long and twenty feet high, has the following inscription:

> SACRED TO THE MEMORY OF/NATHANAEL GREEN ESQUIRE/A NATIVE OF THE STATE OF RHODE ISLAND/WHO DIED ON THE 19TH OF JUNE 1786/LATE MAJOR GENERAL IN THE SERVICE OF THE U.S./AND COMMANDER OF THEIR ARMY IN THE SOUTHERN DEPARTMENT.

"Esquire" was at that time a term of respect for gentlemen, and did not necessarily indicate that the person was an attorney.

Congress appropriated $50,000 for the thirteen-foot bronze equestrian statue of Major General Nathanael Greene that stands at Maryland and Massachusetts avenues in Stanton Park. *Photo by Janet L. Greentree.*

In 1930, the entire statue was toppled from its pedestal during a severe storm, but was undamaged and returned to position (Goode: 84).

The sculptor, Henry Kirke Brown, also created four of the sculptures in Statuary Hall, among them one of Nathanael Greene, and two statues of Lincoln in New York City. Brown's other credits include the less impressive equestrian statue of Winfield Scott at Massachusetts Avenue and 16th Street, N.W.

About twenty-five years after the dedication of the Greene statue in the District, the general's remains were located in Congressional Cemetery in Savannah, Georgia, following a search spearheaded by Colonel Asa B. Gardiner of the Rhode Island Society of the Cincinnati. On November 14, 1902, Greene and his son, George Washington Greene, were re-interred beneath a monument to the general in Savannah's Johnson Square.

Location: Maryland and Massachusetts avenues, N.W., in Stanton Park.

Peace Monument

Washington, D.C. is replete with bronze or marble avatars perched upon lofty pedestals, and surrounded or flanked by secondary sculptures exuding Classical or historical allusions. Often these peripheral figures are situated at the base of the monument, even below the feet of the heroic icon that towers above both them and passersby. But in at least one case, one of these lesser representations has quietly usurped the original nomenclature of the monument.

The Peace Monument, on the West Capitol Grounds, is all symbolism and allegory, and without the identifying inscriptions, would offer few clues as to the subject. The United States, represented as a weeping woman, is crying on the shoulder of a somber lady, representing History, who holds a book in her left hand. On the book's cover are the words "They died that their country might live." Both women are draped in togas. Beneath them is Victory, head bowed slightly, holding aloft a wreath in her right hand. Another wreath is carved into the face of the pedestal, above and behind her. At her feet, Mars and Neptune – the Roman gods of war and the sea – recline casually. The two are more cherubic than fearsome. Opposite Victory, on the east side of the pedestal, is the figure of Peace.

The base of the monument is made of blue granite, and was designed by Edward Clark, architect of the Capitol. An inscription reads:

"In Memory of the Officers, Seamen, and Marines of the United States Navy Who Fell in Defense of the Union and Liberty of Their Country, 1861-1865." Admiral David D. Porter, Superintendent of the United States Naval Academy and step brother of the late Admiral David G. Farragut, had always referred to the piece as the Naval Monument. According to U.S. Navy records, 2,260 sailors and Marines were killed in action during the Civil War. Exact figures for Confederate forces are not known.

Like many American expatriate artists of the time, sculptor Franklin Simmons worked out of a studio in Europe, his in Rome. Simmons based his design for the Peace Monument on a drawing that Porter had made. The forty-foot monument was erected in 1877, six years after Porter first came up with the idea. There was never any official dedication ceremony. The cost came to roughly $40,000, half of which was raised by Porter through soliciting donations from naval personnel, and half of which was appropriated by Congress.

Location: Pennsylvania Avenue at 1st Street N.W.

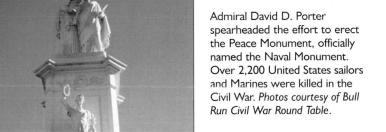

Admiral David D. Porter spearheaded the effort to erect the Peace Monument, officially named the Naval Monument. Over 2,200 United States sailors and Marines were killed in the Civil War. *Photos courtesy of Bull Run Civil War Round Table.*

Robert A. Taft

The son of President William Howard Taft, Robert A. Taft (1889-1953), served three terms as an Ohio senator. A staunch Republican, Taft made three unsuccessful bids for his party's presidential nomination. His memorial is an eleven-foot bronze statue, standing at the base of a 100-foot bell tower designed by architect Douglas W. Orr. Taft's right hand is placed on his stomach, his left hand is at his side, the thumb stuck in the hip pocket of his trousers. The $1 million cost was borne by donations.

New York sculptor Wheeler Williams did a lot of preparation in designing the statue, including interviewing colleagues and family members of the late senator, reading as much about the subject as he could, and modeling the sculpture's stance with the assistance of Taft's sons, Horace and Robert, Jr. Williams went through numerous clay models and several revisions before coming up with a result that was satisfactory to all parties involved. The product of two and a half years of work is a surprisingly plain-looking statue that might depict any middle-aged man, one whose face betrays no hint of emotion. The legs appear to be disproportionately long in relation to the body, and the exaggerated creases in the trousers draw even more attention to this.

Presiding at the April 14, 1959 dedication was President Dwight D. Eisenhower, whose vice president, Richard M. Nixon, formally accepted the memorial. Speeches were given by former president Herbert Hoover, House Speaker Sam Rayburn, Taft's son, William, and several senators and representatives.

At a small ceremony the preceding day, several items of memorabilia were sealed inside the bell tower's cornerstone, including a microfilm listing the names of the 10,000 donors.

Location: Constitution Avenue and 1st Street.

A 100-foot bell tower looms beyond Wheeler Williams's sculpture of the late Senator Robert A. Taft. *Photos by Maureen R. Quinn.*

Ulysses S. Grant

Seated stoically on his horse, the serene Cincinnatus, the slouching figure of Ulysses S. Grant impassively surveys the pandemonium erupting below him. The general's hands rest on his hips, while his features are strained, haggard, yet indefatigable. Dressed in a heavy coat and with his wide-brimmed hat pulled down close to his eyes, Grant is a beacon of tranquility amidst a sea of turmoil. Following the Civil War, Union veterans recalled seeing their unflappable commander occasionally whittling during battles.

Flanking the general is an artillery crew, lurching forward into battle. Four horses bearing three riders lug a mounted cannon behind them, while three artillerists ride in the caisson next to the big gun. Opposite them is a seven-man cavalry group, among them a bugler and a flag bearer. The raised right hand of the commander leading the charge grips the pommel of a sword, the blade having been broken off by vandals. To his right, a rider is being crushed beneath his fallen steed.

Grant is surrounded by four reclining lions on their own marble pedestals, the only allegorical aspects of this lurid bronze battle sculpture. Two of the lions face the direction of Grant and his horse, while two look the opposite way.

The various components of the Grant Memorial were installed as they were completed, a piecemeal process not uncommon in the erection of monuments. The lions were added first, in 1908, followed by the artillery crew in 1912, the cavalry in 1916, and Grant himself in 1921. Grant's marble pedestal is forty feet high, seventy-one feet wide and 252 feet long.

The second largest sculpture group in the world, Henry Merwin Schrady's masterpiece is the result of twenty years of painstaking research. The New York sculptor had a personal connection to the eighteenth president. Shrady's father, George, acted as physician to Grant in the former general's final days. Assisting Shrady in the design of the memorial was architect Edward Pearce Casey.

Many prominent sculptors who had submitted entries in the 1902 contest held by the Grant Memorial Commission were openly jealous when Shrady's design was chosen. Among the envious competitors was Charles Henry Niehaus, who had sculpted the statues of Samuel Hahnemann, at Massachusetts Avenue and 16th Street, and John Paul Jones, at 17th Street and Independence Avenue. Niehaus's vitriolic correspondence, which the petulant artist had penned to the Grant Memorial Commission even prior to their official selection of Shrady, was laced with accusations of favoritism and bribery (Jacob: 41).

The official unveiling came on April 27, 1922, the 100th anniversary of Grant's birth. Weakened from two decades of exhaustive work and a recent bout with influenza, Shrady had died two months earlier. Two years later, bronze bas-relief panels were added to the sides of Grant's marble pedestal. Sculpted by Sherry Fry, the panels depict Union infantry.

In 1864, Union forces under Grant numbered over half a million. His army fought Robert E. Lee's to a standstill at Petersburg, Virginia. After nine long months, Grant was finally victorious, and went on to occupy Richmond. A good friend of fellow Ohioan William T. Sherman, Grant was a poor businessmen, an inefficient president, and a great soldier. Mary Todd Lincoln disliked him, implying that his military triumphs had been, in effect, Pyrrhic victories.

Location: Union Square, in the Capitol Hill district, east end of the Reflecting Pool.

This photograph shows the incredible detail of the cavalry group in the Grant Memorial. *Photo courtesy of Bull Run Civil War Round Table.*

Henry Merwin Schrady spent twenty years working on the Ulysses S. Grant Memorial. Ironically, the sculptor died two months before the dedication. *Photo courtesy of Bull Run Civil War Round Table.*

Veterans of Foreign Wars Memorial

Nowhere was the flourish of patriotism that characterized America's bicentennial more evident than in the nation's capital. Far from being obscured in the annals of history by the countless other ceremonies that year, the dedication of the Torch of Freedom in the summer of 1976 helped guarantee its place for posterity. Although other monuments had been erected to individuals, members of certain divisions, and branches of service, acknowledged Veterans of Foreign Wars Commander-in-Chief Thomas C. Walker, this was the capital's only all-inclusive military tribute – recognizing those who had served in all of the branches of the military, throughout all of their country's wars. His remarks followed the keynote address of Secretary of Defense Donald H. Rumsfeld, who alluded to the old adage that freedom is not free.

"It is secure today but it is never permanently guaranteed," Rumsfeld said. "That is for each generation, in turn" (VFW).

The monument consists of a thirty-six-foot gilded bronze shaft atop an eight-foot white marble pedestal. On each of the shaft's three sides are four five-foot by six-foot bronze bas-relief panels, depicting scenes from the American Revolution, the War of 1812, the Civil War, the Spanish-American War, World War I, World War II, the Korean War, and the Vietnam War. One-fourth of the panels are dedicated to the Civil War, a conflict with more artistic representation in the capital than any other event in American history. These scenes include Lee's surrender to Grant at Appomattox Courthouse, a small group of Confederate cavalry, and a Union artillery crew standing beside a cannon. Each bronze panel weighs 2,000 pounds. On either side of the marble pedestal are bronze emblems with the insignia of the five branches of service. Beneath that is a bronze hemisphere of the world, encircled by the names of major campaigns of the eight wars represented. Crowning the shaft is an urn, from which sprouts a golden flame – the "Torch of Freedom."

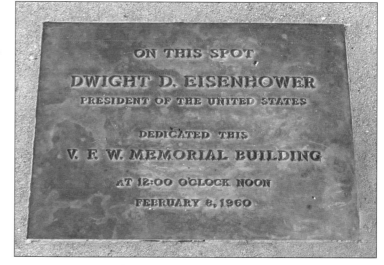

A memorial plaque at the Torch of Freedom. *Photo courtesy of VFW.*

"1776 1976" is inscribed on the front of the marble base, flanked by bronze medallions bearing the insignia of the Veterans of Foreign Wars and the Ladies Auxiliary. Beneath that are the words:

> Out of the past so great to build a greater future in honor and memory of the veterans of all America's wars who by their service kept the TORCH OF FREEDOM burning. This monument is dedicated by the Veterans of Foreign Wars of the U.S. and the Ladies Auxiliary of the V.F.W. in honor of all who have served, their parents, wives, and children.

Sculptor Felix W. de Weldon explained that he was inspired by a similar monument in Athens, Greece. De Weldon, a World War II naval veteran, was already well-known for the Iwo Jima Memorial in Arlington National Cemetery, in addition to nearly thirty other commemorative works. De Weldon received a $250,000 commission for the Veterans of Foreign Wars Memorial, one-fifth of which was donated by The Ladies Auxiliary. The names of contributors were inscribed in a book that was placed inside the base.

Location: VFW Memorial Building, at the trisection of 2nd Street and Constitution and Maryland avenues, two blocks from the Capitol.

On each of the shaft's three sides are four five-foot by six-foot bronze bas-relief panels, depicting scenes from America's various wars. *Photo courtesy of VFW.*

The VFW's "Torch of Freedom," dedicated during the nation's bicentennial. *Photo courtesy of VFW.*

Winged Statue of Freedom atop the Capitol Dome

For many Washingtonians, the old wooden dome of the Capitol was an eyesore, so they were much relieved about its replacement in 1850 with the nine million pound cast iron one that has graced the building ever since. That same year, two new wings were added to the Capitol. Still, something seemed to be missing, as if the sturdy new structure cried out audibly for further adornment. The answer was the embodiment of the ideal on which the country had been founded three-quarters of a century ago.

Weighing over seven tons, the nineteen-foot statue is made of five separate pieces of bronze. Freedom is personified as a woman holding a sheathed sword in her right hand, and a shield and a wreath in her left hand. She is clad in flowing robes, and wears what appears to be a Native American-style headdress, but is actually a helmet encircled with stars and capped with an eagle's head, which sprouts long feathers. Sculptor Thomas Crawford's 1855 plans called for her to be adorned with a cap similar to those worn by freed Roman slaves, but future president of the Confederacy Jefferson Davis, who was then Franklin Pierce's Secretary of War, objected vehemently, claiming that this was some sort of abolitionist propaganda intended to demean the South. Crawford stood down, revising the design accordingly. The base of the statue is a globe encircled by a banner reading "E Pluribus Unum." Ironically, the casting for

"Freedom" was made by slaves in 1862. Another of Crawford's better-known works is the bas-relief for the north pediment of the Capitol, depicting lady America surrounded by twelve allegorical figures.

Crawford was an ambitious artist who perhaps took on a bit more than he could handle, evidenced by the fact that several of his projects were left unfinished at the time of his death in 1857. In 1849, he was commissioned to create a monument for the city of Richmond, Virginia. Crawford's design called for an equestrian statue of George Washington atop a towering plinth, surrounded by statues of six other famous Virginians on lower pedestals. The six subordinate sculptures were completed after Crawford's death by Randolph Rogers.

Unfortunately, Crawford did not live to see Freedom mounted on top of the Capitol Dome in December of 1863, either. After his death from cancer, his widow, Louisa, arranged to have a model of the statue transported by ship from her late husband's studio in Rome to Washington, D.C.

In 1993, Freedom was temporarily removed for cleaning. Today, she surveys the city from a vantage point of 288 feet.

Location: Atop the Capitol Dome, North Capitol and East Capitol avenues.

Thomas Crawford's winged statue of Freedom surveys the capital from a vantage point of 288 feet. The nineteen-foot statue is made of five separate pieces of bronze. *Photos by Janet L. Greentree.*

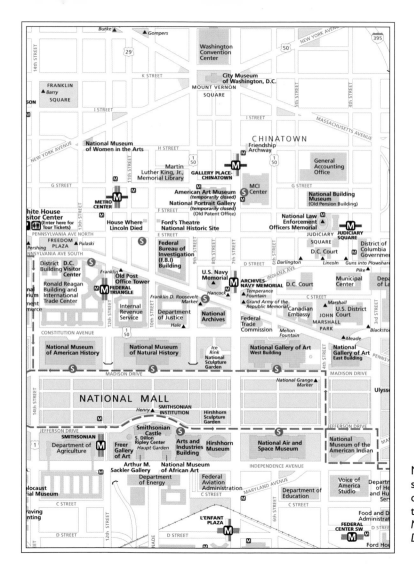

2

Map locating most of the statues and monuments discussed in this section of the guide. *Map courtesy of the National Park Service, U.S. Department of the Interior.*

From the National Mall to Chinatown

Albert Pike

In 1934, a statue of Robert E. Lee was placed in the Capitol's Statuary Hall, but there is only one outdoor statue in Washington, D.C. memorializing a Confederate general: that of Albert Pike, on 3rd and D streets, N.W. Erected in 1901, this bronze likeness is the work of Gaetano Trentanove. Like many sculptors of the time, Trentanove had a studio in Florence, Italy, which probably boasted more artists than any other city in the world. In his 1903 book, *The History of American Sculpture,* Lorado Taft explains that this phenomenon was especially common in the early nineteenth century:

Almost without exception these sculptors of the first half of the century were animated by a single desire, — to get to Italy as soon as possible ... Their own country afforded neither sculptural instruction nor example (5).

Taft also points out that Italy had a plentiful supply of high-quality sculpting materials, such as the pink granite quarried in Carrerra.

The fact that Pike was a Confederate general caused some controversy, but the memorial was commissioned by his fellow Freemasons, not Confederate veterans. Despite protests by the Grand Army of the Republic (see entry on Grand Army of the Republic Monument, p. 41), Congress passed a joint resolution on April 9, 1898 granting permission for a monument of Pike to be erected on public grounds in the District of Columbia.

The only reference to Pike's dubious military career is the word "soldier," inscribed around the base of the eleven-foot statue, along with "scholar," "philosopher," "jurist," "orator," "author," and "poet." He is depicted as a bearded, middle-aged man-of-letters, carrying a stack of books under his left arm. His left foot is slightly forward, and his right hand is partially raised, as if he is gesturing to make a point. Pike's name is inscribed directly beneath him. The goddess of Masonry is seated below Pike, on the second tier of the pedestal. Her right hand holds up the banner of the Scottish Rite, which depicts a crowned, two-headed eagle beneath a field of thirty-three stars. Trentanove completed the piece in four years.

Though born in Boston in 1809, Pike threw his support behind the South when civil war broke out. After openly criticizing the Confederacy, he was incarcerated and forced to resign his commission as brigadier general. He died in 1891 in Washington, D.C., where he had lived and practiced law for the past twenty-three years. From 1859 until his death, Pike served as the Sovereign Grand Commander of the Supreme Grand Council of the 33rd Degree of the Ancient and Accepted Scottish Rite of Free-Masonry, Southern Jurisdiction of the United States. The Southern Jurisdiction encompassed all but fifteen states, and included several foreign jurisdictions, as well. Pike was a shrewd lawyer, a prolific writer, and an accomplished linguist.

The unveiling of the $15,000 monument was held on May 31, 1901, the Supreme Council's 100th anniversary. Frederick Webber, Secretary General to the Council, tread lightly on the issue of Pike's Confederate sympathies, stating, "... although he may have been arrayed against the government in the [C]ivil [W]ar, in peace he was its strong and earnest friend" (Ancient & Accepted Scottish Rite of Free-Masonry: 138). As part of the dedication ceremony, the monument was tested with a square, level, and plumb to insure the accuracy of its specifications, and the granite base was anointed with corn, wine, and oil.

Location: 3rd and D streets, N.W.

The dedication of the Albert Pike Memorial, May 31, 1901. *Photos courtesy of The Supreme Council, 33°, Southern Jurisdiction, USA.*

Andrew Jackson Downing Memorial Urn

This four-foot marble memorial urn, which sits atop a pedestal, is in memory of the architect who landscaped the Mall, which does not resemble his original concept anymore, due to a redesign project by the Commission of Fine Arts about 100 years ago. In 1972, the urn was moved from the grounds of The National Museum of Natural History to its present location. The urn, which was created in 1856 by Robert E. Launitz, has a fluted, expanding base, and is carved with plant-like designs.

Andrew Jackson Downing was a prominent architect, who authored several books on gardening and landscaping, among them *Cottage Residences* (1847), *A Treatise on the Theory and Practice of Landscape Gardening* (1849), *The Architecture of Country Houses* (1850), *Hints to Persons About Building in the Country* (posthumously, 1859). His promising career was cut short by a fatal boating accident in 1852, when he was thirty-seven.

Location: The Smithsonian Castle, Independence Avenue and 10th Street.

The Andrew W. Mellon Memorial Fountain pays tribute to the wealthy Pittsburgh industrialist whose donation of European art, coupled with a generous monetary contribution, established the National Gallery of Art. *Photo by Maureen R. Quinn.*

Andrew W. Mellon Memorial Fountain

In designing the Andrew W. Mellon Memorial Fountain, architect Otto R. Eggers drew his inspiration from a similar fountain in Genoa, Italy (Goode: 144). At the May 9, 1952 dedication, Secretary of the Interior Oscar Chapman stated that a fountain was a perfect tribute, implying that there were already far too many statues in Washington, D.C. Also in attendance that day were Pennsylvania Governor John S. Fine and Mellon's son and daughter. The fountain was turned on immediately following the dedication ceremony, and Chapman declared that it would remain so year round.

The Andrew W. Mellon Memorial Fountain pays tribute to the wealthy Pittsburgh industrialist whose donation of European art, coupled with a generous monetary contribution, established the National Gallery of Art. *Photo by Maureen R. Quinn.*

Sculpted by Sidney Waugh, the fountain consists of three concentric bronze bowls, the outermost of which is engraved with Zodiac symbols which have been carefully located to correspond with the position of heavenly bodies at key seasonal intervals. Warm weather often finds children wading barefoot in the twenty-five-foot diameter pool that forms the base, as clear cataracts cascade over the edges of the triple font. Fountains in the capital are turned off during colder months, but even without the continuous ebullience for which it was originally intended, the fountain manages to instill in viewers a quiet contemplation, and an aesthetic appreciation in even the most inartistically-inclined. The $300,000 cost was borne by private donors, mostly friends and associates of Mellon.

A wealthy Pittsburgh industrialist, Mellon (1855-1937) was Secretary of the Treasury from 1921 through 1931, under the administrations of presidents Warren G. Harding, Calvin Coolidge, and Herbert Hoover. Afterwards, he served briefly as ambassador to Great Britain. From his extensive travels overseas, Mellon had amassed an astounding collection of European artwork by the foremost masters. His donated works of art – consisting of 128 pieces – formed the original collection of the capital's National Gallery of Art when the institution opened in 1941.

Location: Constitution and Pennsylvania avenues, N.W., in the Federal Triangle.

Benjamin Banneker Fountain

Benjamin Banneker was born on his parents' Maryland tobacco farm in 1731. As a youth, he developed a keen interest in math and astronomy. He had learned to read from his grandmother, Molly, and had a few years of formal schooling. As a young man, he constructed a working clock after taking apart and studying a pocket watch which a neighbor had given him. Between 1792 and 1797, Banneker published an almanac for farmers. In 1791 he and Andrew Ellicott were appointed to survey the site selected by George Washington for Federal City, in the District of Columbia.

An educated, free black, Banneker was an anomaly for his time. His father and grandfather had been freed slaves, and the plight of fellow blacks was always on his mind. In 1792 he composed an eloquent letter to Secretary of State Thomas Jefferson, decrying the evils of slavery. Jefferson's response was cordial and even sympathetic, but indicated that the future president had no intention of pursuing the matter any further. Banneker died in 1806, at the age of seventy-five.

Location: Benjamin Banneker Park.

Benjamin Franklin

Washington, D.C. sculptor Jacques Jouvenal strove as much for authenticity as for artistry when he sculpted the statue of Benjamin Franklin (1706-1790) that stands at Pennsylvania Avenue and 12th Street. The location in front of the old post office alludes to Franklin's position as joint deputy postmaster, which he held from 1753 to 1774, and the coat in which he is draped was closely modeled from an actual garment that he was known to wear. Franklin's right hand is raised in a somewhat conciliatory gesture, as if he is trying politely to make a point to a stubborn listener. In his left hand Franklin is holding a partially-furled scroll. The intent was to depict the diplomat and statesman addressing the British delegation at Versailles in 1783, when he negotiated the treaty that officially ended the Revolutionary War. Standing eight-feet tall upon an eleven-foot granite pedestal, the statue was designed by Ernst Plassman, who also designed a bronze statue of Franklin in New York City in 1872.

Stilson Hutchins, founder of the *Washington Post*, erected this memorial to Benjamin Franklin in 1889. *Photo by Maureen R. Quinn.*

On the south side of the pedestal, just below the statue, is the name "FRANKLIN." The words "PRINTER," "PHILOSOPHER," "PATRIOT," and "PHILANTHROPIST" appear on the respective four sides of the pedestal, in the center. Near the base is the inscription "PRESENTED TO THE NATIONAL CAPITAL/BY/STILSON HUTCHINS." A bronze plate on the base notes the date of dedication, and the names of the sculptor, designer, and stone cutter who collaborated on the project, as well as the names of Washington, D.C.'s three commissioners at the time. From the base to the top of Franklin's head is about twenty feet, and the entire memorial weighs over twelve tons.

The January 17, 1889 dedication was on Franklin's 183rd birthday. According to the *Washington Post*, a pouring rain pelted the crowd during the unveiling, but as soon as Franklin's great-granddaughter pulled the cord that drew back the flag, exposing the statue, the deluge subsided. She was given the ceremonial flag as a gift. Also present at the unveiling were three of Franklin's great-great grandchildren.

New Hampshire native Stilson Hutchins, who founded the *Washington Post* and three other newspapers, erected the statue as a tribute to his fellow journalist.

Location: Pennsylvania Avenue and 12th Street, in the Federal Triangle.

Casimir Pulaski

In choosing to leave Poland and fight for American independence, Count Casimir Pulaski may have felt somewhat vindicated by helping to secure for the Colonies what he had failed to secure for his native country. Poland had long been and would long continue to be a lightning rod for invasions and partitions, and would see little relief until over 200 years after Pulaski's untimely demise. Benjamin Franklin, ever the consummate diplomat, arranged for Pulaski's American expedition after meeting with him in Paris. In 1777 the count arrived in the Colonies, and enlisted at once in the Continental Army. Already an experienced officer, he was made a brigadier general, and given his own cavalry command, leading a mounted force known as "Pulaski's Legion." A friend and colleague of generals Washington and Lafayette, Pulaski served with distinction, inspiring both the deepest respect and affection from his men. His stint with the American military was short-lived, however. He was mortally wounded at the Battle of Savannah, Georgia, in October 1777, and died two days later, at the age of thirty-two.

Thousands turned out for the May 11, 1910, ceremony dedicating the memorial to Polish count Casimir Pulaski, who fought for the freedom of both his native land and the United States. *Photo by Janet L. Greentree.*

An eight-foot bronze statue of Pulaski sits atop an oblong granite pedestal in Freedom Plaza. On the front of the pedestal are Pulaski's name, along with his date and place of death. Pulaski is dressed in a Polish cavalry uniform, and draped in a long cloak. A fur cap rests on his head. Sculptor Kasimiriez Chodzinski received $40,000 for the piece.

The memorial was dedicated May 11, 1910. Prior to an address by President William Howard Taft, John F. Smulski of Chicago told the crowd that it was appropriate that those who fought for Polish independence, albeit unsuccessfully, also lent a hand in the cause of American independence. The two countries essentially shared the same dreams, the same goal of freedom.

The guest of honor was Count Francis Pulaski, who had traveled from Poland to attend the ceremony. He spoke a few brief words about the contributions of his ancestor, and thanked the American people for "a magnificent tribute."

Following the dedication, the huge crowd of Polish-Americans, veterans, spectators, and dignitaries made its way to Lafayette Park, where a 4:00 p.m. dedication of the Thaddeus Kosciuszko statue was scheduled.

Location: Pennsylvania Avenue and 13th Street, in Freedom Plaza.

The Future and The Past

Although they do not at first suggest inconsistency, the two twelve-foot limestone statues by the Pennsylvania Avenue entrance to the National Archives building represent a melange of three different milieus – English Renaissance, ancient Roman, and far Eastern. The accompanying inscriptions are from Confucius and Shakespeare, yet convey essentially the same meaning. A collaboration between sculptor Robert Aitken and

architect John Russell Pope, the statues complement each other with their symmetrical opposition, conveying a sense of balance reminiscent of a pair of giant bookends. They were installed in 1935.

To the left is Future, a plain-looking, hooded young woman with an open book in her lap. Her left arm is draped over the back of the chair in which she is sitting, and she is clutching several papers in her left hand. Beneath her is a quote from the Bard: "What is past is prologue."

Her counterpart, a balding, bearded, middle-aged man has a closed book in his lap, and his right arm rests on the back of his chair. His right hand holds what appears to be a furled scroll. The inscription below him – "Study the past" – is from the aforementioned Chinese philosopher.

Location: National Archives Building, Pennsylvania Avenue and 8th Street, N.W.

The Future and The Past appropriately flank the entrance to the National Archives. *Photos by Maureen R. Quinn.*

George Gordon Meade

This impressive marble memorial by Philadelphia sculptor Charles Grafly features Major General George Gordon Meade and seven allegorical figures, representing War, Loyalty, Chivalry, Fame, Energy, Progress, and Military Courage, congregated atop a rounded pedestal. Depicted as nearly-nude youths, three figures stand between Meade and War on either side. War, who resembles the Angel of Death, is directly opposite Meade and facing the other direction, as if purposefully turning his back on the heroic general. Clinging to War's right and left arms are Military Courage and Energy, respectively. In between the two long tablets that War holds in either hand is a fearsome, two-edged sword. War is wearing an armor breastplate, and his sandaled feet protrude from beneath the tablets, on which are inscribed the names of Meade's battles.

Meade is clad in full uniform – double-breasted coat, gloves, and knee-high boots – a sword swinging at his left side. To his right is the young male figure representing Loyalty, and to his left, the young woman representing Chivalry. Both are helping to remove the long cloak – symbolic of the mantle of war – draped over Meade's back. Rising above Meade's head is an emblem with an eagle in the center, which is supported by two semicircles composed of upright feathers. Large, blossoming flowers sprout beneath Meade's feet.

The George Gordon Meade Memorial by Philadelphia sculptor Charles Grafly. *Photo by Tatiana Madise.*

An inscription at the base of the pedestal reads:

THE COMMONWEALTH OF PENNSYLVANIA TO MAJOR GENERAL GEORGE GORDON MEADE WHO COMMANDED THE UNION FORCES AT GETTYSBURG.

The design, site selection, and eventual erection of the memorial was decided by both the Meade Memorial Commission, appointed by the governor of Pennsylvania, and the Washington, D.C.-based Commission of Fine Arts. The $200,000 cost was borne by the state of Pennsylvania, which presented the memorial as a gift to the nation's capital. Both President Calvin Coolidge and Pennsylvania governor John S. Fisher spoke at the memorial's October 19, 1927 dedication.

The initial planning for the memorial began in 1915. John W. Frazier, who was with Meade at Gettysburg, served as secretary to the Meade Memorial commission. Members of the Fine Arts Commission found Frazier to be stubborn, argumentative, and plain mean-spirited (Jacob: 55-56). They were almost relieved when he died in 1918, but it was still another nine years before their work would be done.

Meade, who was born in Cadiz, Spain, led the Army of the Potomac to victory against Robert E. Lee's forces at the Battle of Gettysburg, Pennsylvania, which took place from July 1 through July 3, 1863. Meade died in 1872, and was interred in Philadelphia's famous Laurel Hill Cemetery.

Location: Pennsylvania Avenue between 3rd and 4th streets, N.W., in the Federal Triangle.

Grand Army of the Republic Monument

The death of 109-year-old Albert Woolson on August 2, 1956 was the end of a living legacy embodying part of the greatest struggle that the country had ever witnessed, and the most prominent and powerful veterans' organization created to date. Woolson, who was mustered into Company C of the First Minnesota Volunteer Heavy Artillery at the age of seventeen, was both the last surviving Union Civil War veteran, as well as the last surviving member of the Grand Army of the Republic (see John A. Logan Memorial, p. 183). In a 1957 interview, 110-year-old John Salling of Virginia claimed to be the last surviving Confederate veteran. Salling died two years later, and his claim has been disputed by some.

Starting out as a fraternity for Union veterans, the GAR lobbied effectively for pensions and hiring preferences for members, provided financial assistance to veterans' families, and gradually transformed into a political juggernaut for the Republican party. Six years before Woolson's passing, the organization held its final encampment in Indiana, and officially disbanded.

But the efforts of an aging group of GAR members had engendered another legacy in 1909, not in flesh and blood, but in granite and bronze. A striated shaft with sculptures set into shallow alcoves on each of the three sides, the GAR Monument personifies the ideals "Fraternity, Charity, and Loyalty" – the group's motto – and memorializes founder Benjamin Franklin Stephenson. Stephenson, who died in 1871, had served as a surgeon in the 14th Illinois Volunteer Infantry during the Civil War. The sculptor for the bronze figures was John Massey Rhind, a Scotsman who had come to America twenty years earlier.

On the front of the monument, which faces south, are the figures of a Union soldier and sailor – representing Fraternity. The soldier holds a rifle in his right hand, its butt resting on the ground. He is stepping slightly forward, his left foot overlapping the base of the alcove. The sailor holds a furled American flag in his right hand. The eagle atop the flagpole juts out a foot or so above the top of the alcove. Beneath the pair is a bronze bas-relief bust of Stephenson. On the northeast façade is Loyalty – a female warrior – leaning on a large, triangular shield. Her right hand holds a great sword, its tip resting on the ground. The inscription beneath her reads: "Who Knew No Glory But His Country's Good." The third figure, Charity, stands at the northwest façade. She is depicted as a woman draped in a robe and cape. Her left hand rests gently on the shoulder of a child nestled against her side. Inscribed at the base is "The greatest of these is charity."

A stirring tribute to the late, great Grand Army of the Republic, which at one time was the largest organization for Union veterans of the Civil War. *Photo courtesy of Bull Run Civil War Round Table.*

The cost of the memorial was about $45,000, two-thirds of which was raised by the GAR. Among those attending the July 3, 1909 dedication were President William Howard Taft, Rhind, and current Commander-in-Chief of the GAR Colonel Henry M. Nevius, who was the main speaker.

Location: Pennsylvania Avenue and 7th Street, in Indiana Plaza.

Heritage and Guardianship

A common theme occurs in the statuary that flanks the steps of the respective entrances to the National Archives Building. Similar to Robert Aitken's Future and Past statues, Heritage and Guardianship are a female and male pair that both quietly emphasize the relationship between what has been and what is yet to be. They are gentle reminders that the former is often a harbinger of the latter. Both are eight feet in height, made of limestone, and seated atop huge granite blocks inscribed with appropriate quotations.

Heritage is a bare-chested, short-haired young woman whose lower torso is draped in loose-hanging garments. Her smooth, serene countenance is pointed slightly to her left, as if observing visitors passing between her and her male counterpart on the opposite side. In her right hand is a naked male infant standing in front of a sheaf of wheat. The inscription beneath her, surrounded by agricultural designs carved into the granite, reads: "THE HERITAGE OF THE PAST/IS THE SEED THAT BRINGS FORTH/THE HARVEST OF THE FUTURE."

Sculptor James Earle Fraser, who completed the Authority of Law and Contemplation of Justice sculptures for the Supreme Court Building the same year, came up with the quotation.

On the front of Guardianship's pedestal is a stern, silent warning.
Photo by Maureen R. Quinn.

Guardianship is a bit more rugged, a bit wary as he looks askance at passersby. The chiseled muscles of his chest and stomach suggest raw power. He appears ready at a moment's notice to don the large, plumed helmet in his right hand, or to draw the sheathed sword clasped behind the fasces on his left. A Roman symbol of authority, the fasces is represented as a bundle of sticks bound with a cord, and with an axe blade protruding from the top. The fasces appears in numerous stat-ues throughout the capital. The adoption of this symbol by Mussolini's regime in the 1930s forever altered its once benign denotation. Inscribed beneath Guardianship are Thomas Jefferson's words: "ETERNAL VIGILANCE/IS THE PRICE OF LIBERTY."

Heritage and Guardianship were erected in 1935. Architect James Russell Pope assisted with the design.

Location: National Archives Building, southern entrance, Constitution Avenue and 7th Street.

On the front of Guardianship's pedestal is a stern, silent warning. *Photo by Maureen R. Quinn.*

John Marshall

From his perch above Constitution Avenue and 4th Street in Judiciary Square, Justice Marshall sits in a simple armchair, draped in his judicial robes, a book in his left hand. Marshall's right hand is extended, as if beckoning someone to approach. Like so many memorials in the nation's capital, this one skillfully blends Classicism with American history. The north side of the granite pedestal depicts Minerva, the Roman goddess of wisdom (whose Greek counterpart is Athena), dictating the Constitution to the new nation. Opposite Minerva is a panel depicting Victory laying down her weapons of war.

The United States Bar Association erected this memorial in 1884 to honor the fourth Chief Justice of the Supreme Court, who had died nearly fifty years earlier. Sculptor William Wetmore Story was the son of Joseph Story, who served as an associate justice in Marshall's court. Story completed the five-foot bronze statue in his Rome studio in 1883. There is a replica of the statue in front of the Philadelphia Museum of Art.

Marshall was appointed to the Supreme Court by President John Adams, and served from 1801 until his death in 1835, longer than any other Chief Justice. At the time of his appointment, Marshall was also Adams's Secretary of State. Prior to that, he had represented his home state of Virginia while the United States was under the Articles of Confederation, as well as after the ratification of the Constitution. He had been a captain in the Continental Army during the Revolutionary War, and was among the troops stationed at Valley Forge in the winter of 1777 to 1778. An admirer of fellow Virginian George Washington, Marshall wrote a detailed biography of his late commander-in-chief around 1807.

Chief Justice John Marshall. *Photo by Franz Jantzen, Collection of the Supreme Court of the United States.*

Marshall was a firm defender of the Constitution's sovereignty over individual states' laws, and he presided over several cases which established this precedent. In addition, he reinforced the notion that the Supreme Court's role was to interpret the law, not legislate.

Location: Constitution Avenue and 4th Street, in John Marshall Park, Judiciary Square.

Joseph Henry

From the vantage point of someone standing directly in front of the nine-foot heroic bronze of Joseph Henry, the rosette window on the building behind Henry seems to frame his head. The effect is like a halo, or the beams of light emanating from saints' heads in old paintings. This was either shrewd planning on the part of the designer, or a remarkable coincidence. Whatever the case, the view is most impressive.

Henry stands at the entrance to the Smithsonian Castle, the building that housed the collection of the original museum and that now serves as the institution's administrative offices. In his right hand Henry is holding the front of the scholarly robes in which he is garbed, while his left hand rests on an electromagnet. William Wetmore Story sculpted the statue for an April 19, 1883 unveiling, and jobbers worked up to the last minute, finishing the concrete foundation just days before the unveiling. Band

leader John Philip Sousa wrote "The Transit of Venus March" specifically for the dedication ceremony. Many proposed monuments have languished in the planning stages for decades, but Henry's was erected less than five years after his death. In 1880, Congress had appropriated $15,000 for the Henry memorial.

An eminent scientist and researcher, Henry became the first secretary, or director, of the Smithsonian Institution in 1846. He remained in that capacity for the rest of his life, living and working at the castle for the next thirty-two years. His many professional affiliations included serving as president of both the American Association for the Advancement of Science – which he founded – and the National Academy of Sciences (Goode: 259). As chairman of the United States Lighthouse Board, he worked to develop better methods of signaling ships, with emphasis on better fuels for lighthouse lanterns and improved illumination techniques. In addition to his pioneering work on the electromagnet, which included numerous experiments and discoveries in the field, Henry devoted considerable time to studying the surface of the sun. Prior to coming to the Smithsonian, Henry taught mathematics, and later was hired to teach natural philosophy at the College of New Jersey at Princeton, later known as Princeton University. Henry died in Washington, D.C. in 1878, at the age of eighty, and was interred in his family plot at Oak Hill Cemetery.

A brief biography of Henry published in the following day's edition of *The Washington Post* related that as a boy, Henry preferred lighter subjects, engrossing himself in novels and the theater. The reporter explains that Henry "showed no aptitude for learning or for excellency in the ordinary sports of boy-hood." The course of his life was forever changed when the sixteen-year-old discovered a book titled *Lectures on Experimental Philosophy, Astronomy, and Chemistry*.

Location: Entrance to the Smithsonian Castle, Jefferson Drive and 10th Street.

Lincoln Statue

The first memorial in Washington, D.C. to the martyred sixteenth president, this statue was sculpted by Lot Flannery, an Irish immigrant who owned a stone carving business, and erected in 1868. Planning for the memorial began just two weeks after Lincoln's death. The dedication took place on the third anniversary of Lincoln's assassination. Among the several thousand who turned out were Ulysses S. Grant, William T. Sherman, Winfield Scott Hancock, and President Andrew Johnson. The keynote speech was delivered by Major General Benjamin Brown French. To thwart curious passers-by from seeing the memorial prior to the unveiling, policemen guarded the shrouded statue the night before (Jacob: 69).

Placed in storage in the early 1920s, the marble sculpture almost succumbed to oblivion when clearly overshadowed by Daniel Chester French's massive tribute, the Lincoln Memorial. However, the statue was eventually placed back at C and 4th streets, in Judiciary Square, where it stands today.

Erected in 1868, this statue by Lot Flannery was actually the first "Lincoln Memorial." *Photo courtesy of Bull Run Civil War Round Table.*

Lincoln is shown with his head slightly turned to one side, as if addressing someone standing to his left. He wears a long coat draped over his vest and trousers. His left hand rests on a fasces, a Roman symbol of authority denoted by a bound bundle of sticks with an axe blade protruding from the top. The granite pedestal on which Lincoln stands replaced the much higher, original marble one. Inscribed on the front of the pedestal is simply "LINCOLN."

The statue was funded by contributions from district residents. John T. Ford, in whose theater the president was fatally shot the night of April 15th, 1865, while watching the play *Our American Cousin*, contributed $1,800 (ibid: 68).

Location: C and 4th streets, in Judiciary Square, in front of the Superior Court of Washington, D.C.

Louis Daguerre

Remarkably, the camera traces its origins to the fourth century B.C., when Aristotle noted that a tiny opening in the wall of a dark box projected an image on the opposite interior side. How to make that projected image permanent was what eluded would-be photographers for centuries afterward. In 1839, Louis-Jacques Mande Daguerre (1787-1851) patented a process whereby photographic images could be permanently imprinted upon iodized silver plates. Although early daguerreotypes of-

ten took several minutes to complete, continued research resulted in faster production times and better quality images (Jackson).

Though certainly not undeserving of his place in history, Daguerre has obscured many individuals with whom he should share credit, chief among them his business partner, scientist Nicephore Niepce. Niepce and his brother had been experimenting with lithographs more than thirty years before he and Daguerre, a French artist, met. The fact that Niepce predeceased Daguerre by eight years may have contributed to his being eclipsed by the latter. In addition, Daguerre relied on another scientist, Louis Arago, to present the initial findings to the Academy of Sciences in Paris. Daguerre reasoned that members of the French scientific community would be more inclined to listen to news of scientific advances if those advances were presented by one of their own. But it was not Arago, nor Niepce, nor Aristotle whom the Photographic Association of America honored in 1939.

The memorial features a huge stone ball atop an anvil-shaped pedestal engraved with Daguerre's name. Directly underneath the ball is a bronze bas-relief of Daguerre. Another bronze figure, a woman in a long dress, is placing a wreath around the bust of Daguerre. The wreath extends over the top and behind the ball, as well as down the sides of the pedestal. Sculpted by Jonathan S. Hartley, the memorial was originally located in front of the National Museum.

The dedication was held January 7, 1939 to mark the 100th anniversary of the invention of photography. The ceremony did not draw the huge crowds typical at the unveiling of military monuments, and was attended by about 100 people, among them representatives of the Professional Photographers Association, the White House Photographers Association, the Washington Photographic Council, the State Department, and the French Embassy. After laying a red, white, and blue wreath at the memorial, Washington, D.C. cameraman George Harris gave a brief address.

In 1989, the Daguerre memorial was moved to its present location and rededicated.

Location: F and 7th streets, Gallery Place.

Nathan Hale

When General George Washington called for volunteers to conduct espionage on British forces occupying New York City in the fall of 1776, a twenty-one-year-old former schoolteacher from Coventry, Connecticut, stepped forward without hesitation. Older, more experienced men had been reluctant to take the assignment, but the intrepid young patriot was eager to assist his country in any way that he could. A 1773 graduate of Yale University, Nathan Hale resigned his teaching position to become a lieutenant in the local militia in 1774, and shortly thereafter, was commissioned a captain in the Continental Army. The sixth of twelve children of Richard and Elizabeth Hale, Nathan was a bright, charismatic man who might have led a long, prosperous life. This mission would be his last.

Disguising himself as an itinerant educator seeking a position – a ruse which he should have been able to carry off easily – Hale spent a week gathering information. He was captured when he mistook a boat manned by British troops for an American boat with which he was supposed to rendezvous. A search by his captors revealed incriminating documents, and General William Howe ordered his execution. Hale was hanged from an apple tree the following morning.

The bronze statue of Nathan Hale depicts the martyred patriot stoically awaiting his fate, his hands and feet bound, a peaceful, resigned look upon his fresh face. Noticeably absent is the noose. His legendary last words – "I only regret that I have but one life to lose for my country" – are inscribed around the base. The sculptor for this 1915 memorial was Bela L. Pratt.

The inscription on the granite pedestal reads:

NATHAN HALE/CAPTAIN/ARMY OF THE UNITED STATES/BORN AT COVENTRY CONNECTICUT/JUNE 6 1755/IN THE PERFORMANCE OF HIS/DUTY HE RESIGNED HIS/LIFE A SACRIFICE TO/HIS COUNTRY'S LIBERTY/AT NEW YORK/SEPTEMBER 22 1776.

The statue was originally located in Hale's hometown of Coventry, Connecticut, and later was owned by a New York attorney. When the attorney died in 1945, he willed the statue to the United States government, and it has stood at Constitution Avenue and 9th Street since then (Goode: 158).

Location: Constitution Avenue and 9th Street, in the Federal Triangle.

National Law Enforcement Officers Memorial

Some memorials are deliberately ostentatious, arrogantly proclaiming their overwhelming presence as they shoot skyward, cast their colossal silhouettes against the twilight horizon or conspicuously creep across several acres of land. But their sheer magnitude often overshadows their significance. They become like looming cemetery monuments whose inscriptions have long since faded. Not so with the National Law Enforcement Officers Memorial, which still draws over 150,000 visitors every year.

A large plaza framed by two crescent-shaped granite walls, the memorial is a three-acre park nestled unobtrusively between the east and west buildings of the Washington, D.C. Superior Court, in a section of the capital known as Judiciary Square. Designed by Washington, D.C. architect Davis Buckley, the memorial pays tribute to the more than 16,500 fallen law enforcement officers, whose names are inscribed on the walls. Each wall is 304 feet long, and four feet high. The plaza is flanked by a pair of two and a half-ton bronze lions on the south side, and their female counterparts on the north side. Behind each lioness are several sleeping cubs. Sculpted by Ray Kaskey and George Carr, the lions represent the necessary use of force in upholding the law, while the lionesses symbolize the more congenial aspect of police work, inherent in the concept "to protect and serve."

Opposite an eighty-foot long metro escalator at the plaza's south end is a reflecting pool of corresponding dimensions. An inscription reads "National Law Enforcement Officers' Memorial."

At either side of the north and south entrances to the memorial, by F and E streets respectively, is a glass and metal stand with a book listing the names of officers killed in the line of duty; one book organized alphabetically and the other by jurisdiction. The memorial commemorates not just fallen police, but law enforcement officers on the local, state and federal level, including court officials, tax collectors, sheriffs, deputies, marshals, FBI and Secret Service agents, and prison guards. Private donations funded the memorial's $11 million price tag.

An aerial view of the National Law Enforcement Officers Memorial. *Photo courtesy of NLEOMF.*

One of four lion sculptures created by Ray Kaskey and George Carr. *Photo courtesy of NLEOMF.*

Officers point to a name inscribed on a wall at the National Law Enforcement Officers Memorial. An annual candlelight vigil at the start of National Police Week culminates with the reading of the names of fallen officers. In addition, a Wreathlaying Day takes place every October. *Photo courtesy of NLEOMF.*

Sadly, since the memorial's dedication fourteen years ago, over 4,000 new names have been added to the walls. Beginning in April, new names are engraved into the walls, followed at the end of the month by an Engraving Day ceremony. An annual candlelight vigil at the start of National Police Week culminates with the reading of those names. In addition, a Wreathlaying Day takes place every October.

The earliest known case of a law enforcement officer killed in the line of duty is that of Deputy Sheriff Isaac Smith, who was shot in 1792 by a man whom he was attempting to serve a warrant. Other notable names on the walls include John Wilson, the first black officer killed in the line of duty, in 1871; prison matron Anna Hart, the first female law enforcement officer killed in the line of duty, in 1916; and Dallas policeman J.D. Tippit, gunned down while attempting to apprehend Lee Harvey Oswald (NLEOMF).

Location: 4th and E streets N.W., south of F Street and north of E Street, in between the east and west buildings of the Washington, D.C. Superior Court, in Judiciary Square.

U.S. Navy Memorial

Many visitors walking across the 100-foot diameter granite plaza don't even realize that they are standing on the largest map of the world. Flagpoles flank the Pennsylvania Avenue and 8th Street entrances to the plaza, and the impressive, two-tiered Classical colonnades of the Visitor's Center loom in the northern end.

The original design, submitted to the Commission of Fine Arts in 1982, does not even resemble the memorial's present form. The architects had envisioned a kind of outdoor concert area, a square surrounded on three sides by a cloistered walkway. At the southern end would be an enormous Neo-Classical arch of white marble where Navy bands would perform for spectators seated in the center. A pool was planned for the rear of the square, and naval statuary was to be placed strategically throughout the memorial. After significant revisions, the memorial was dedicated on October 13, 1987, the 212th anniversary of the U.S. Navy. The U.S. Navy Memorial pays tribute to past and present sailors.

The southern half of the plaza features twenty-six thirty-two-inch by thirty-six-inch bronze bas-relief panels, commemorating important events and people in naval history. The project was overseen by Leo C. Irrera of Washington, D.C., who also sculpted the panels honoring Navy SEALS, naval construction battalions, naval reservists, and Commodore Matthew Perry.

The memorial is famous for the seven-foot bronze statue known as "Lone Sailor," sculpted by Stanley Bleifield, a World War II naval veteran from New York City. The Lone Sailor stands with his hands tucked into the pockets of his jacket, his collar raised, a sailor's cap on his head, his packed duffel bag beside him. Perhaps he is contemplating what awaits him, or thinking of loved ones back home. When the statue was cast, small metal parts of eight different ships were poured into the molten bronze. Thus, the Lone Sailor is a stout, metallic mixture of naval vessels from the eighteenth to the twentieth century, among them Admiral David G. Farragut's flagship, the USS *Hartford* (U.S. Navy Memorial Foundation).

During an annual ceremony known as "The Blessing of the Feet," sailors bring buckets of water collected from oceans all over the world, and pour them into the fountains, located to the southeast and southwest of the plaza (Rosales & Job).

Location: Pennsylvania Avenue and 8th Street, in Market Square, across from the National Archives Building.

Stanley Bleifield's "Lone Sailor" in the U.S. Navy Memorial. *Photo by Tatiana Madise.*

U.S. Navy Memorial. *Photo by Maureen R. Quinn.*

U.S. Navy Memorial. *Photos by Maureen R. Quinn.*

U.S. Navy Memorial. *Photos by Maureen R. Quinn.*

William Blackstone

The Founding Fathers were not quite as revolutionary in their ideals and principles as many people have imagined. In drafting the Declaration of Independence, Thomas Jefferson relied heavily on George Mason's recently written Virginia Bill of Rights (see George Mason National Memorial, p. 137), and the writers of the Constitution relied heavily on a work written by English judge Sir William Blackstone (1723-1780). Blackstone, the son of a Cheapside silk merchant, authored his famous *Commentaries on English Law* between 1765 and 1769. This venerable, five-volume work formed the basis of English, and eventually, American law. Blackstone's chapters deal with familiar subjects such as trial by jury, individual rights, and corporate law, as well as those not applicable to the framers of the Constitution – duties of the king, and feudalism, for example. In "Section the First" of his introduction, "On the Study of Law," Blackstone deferentially compares and contrasts ancient Roman and eighteenth century English legal systems:

Without detracting therefore from the real merit which abounds in the imperial law, I hope I may have leave to assert, that if an Englishman must be ignorant of either the one or the other, he had better be a stranger to the Roman than the English institutions (Yale Law School).

In 1925, the American Bar Association commissioned sculptor Paul Wayland Bartlett $50,000 for a statue of the Father of English Law, to be given as a gift to the English Bar Association. Three years later, the Blackstone memorial was unveiled at London's Great Hall of Courts. But Bartlett felt that the statue was too large for that particular venue, so he created a smaller piece.

The nine-foot statue of Blackstone that stands at Constitution Avenue and 3rd Street, N.W. was cast in bronze in 1926 at a foundry in Belgium, by arrangement of Bartlett's wife, and unveiled in 1943. House Bill 2106 appropriated $10,000 for the dedication (Hathaway).

Bartlett's sculpture depicts the Oxford law professor garbed in legal robes and a judge's wig, a volume of his *Commentaries* tucked firmly under his left arm. Inscribed in capital letters on the granite block underneath him is his name.

Location: Constitution Avenue and 3rd Street, N.W., in the Federal Triangle.

Winfield Scott Hancock

Myriad monuments to forgotten men dot the parks, squares, and traffic circles of the sixty-seven-square-mile district that was once known as Federal City. Residents and tourists are hard-pressed to imagine that at one time, thousands of spectators packed tightly around these majestic monoliths for a first glance at some proud sculptor's masterpiece. Braving weather fair and foul, people spilled into the surrounding streets to hear litanies of praise heaped upon those whose bronze namesakes stared down on them from prominent perches, as military bands blasted patriotic tunes, smartly-dressed veterans marched in step, and artillery guns boomed distant salutes. In the weeks, months, and sometimes years that followed, streams of visitors came to pay their respects, but those streams at last subsided to a trickle. On a sweltering May afternoon in 1896, Illinois senator John M. Palmer acknowledged that in spite of all of the pomp and celebration that surrounded the dedication of the memorial to Major General Winfield Scott Hancock, and in spite of Hancock's heroic service to his country, he, too, would suffer the same fate.

But the cheering masses were not thinking that far ahead. Minutes earlier, Hancock's grandson had unveiled sculptor Henry Jackson Ellicott's impressive bronze equestrian statue of the late general. Horse and rider stood erect beneath the blazing spring sun. Inscribed on the side of the tall, oblong pedestal on which they were surmounted was the general's name.

Major General Winfield Scott Hancock, commander of the Army of the Potomac, hero of Gettysburg. Sculpted by Henry Jackson Ellicott. *Photos by Janet L. Greentree.*

Congress appropriated $50,000 for the tribute to the officer who had distinguished himself at numerous Civil War battles, most notably Gettysburg. President Grover Cleveland began the ceremonies by announcing "A grateful government today pays tribute to the memory of one of our country's noblest sons and bravest defenders."

Hancock was an 1844 West Point graduate who served in the Mexican-American War alongside several fellow officers who would become his adversaries fifteen years later. He replaced General Joseph Hooker as commander of the Army of the Potomac in 1863, and his troops participated in heavy fighting on Cemetery Ridge at Gettysburg, inflicting serious casualties on the enemy. During the fighting, Hancock was shot in the leg, but refused to leave the field until he was confident that the enemy's advance had been halted. He was given the moniker "Hancock the Superb" by General George B. McClellan. Following the Civil War, Hancock bore no rancor for his erstwhile enemies, even sympathizing with them to an extent (Joyce). He tried his hand at politics in 1880, losing the presidential election to Republican James A. Garfield, a fellow Civil War general. Hancock died in 1884, less than a week before his sixty-second birthday, and was buried in Norristown, Pennsylvania.

Location: Pennsylvania Avenue and 7th Street, in Market Square.

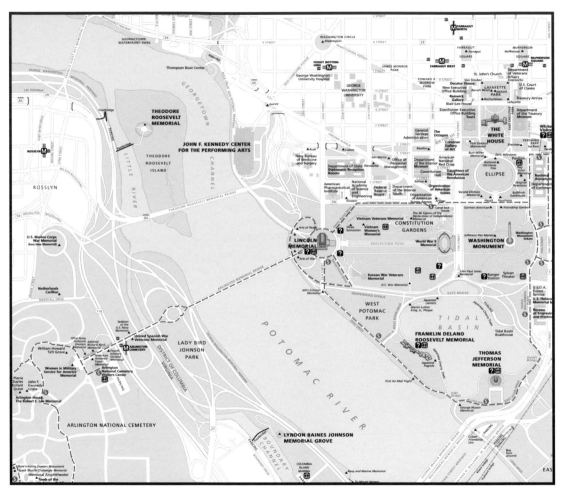

Map locating most of the statues and monuments discussed in all of the subsections in this section of the guide. *Map courtesy of the National Park Service, U.S. Department of the Interior.*

3

From the Washington Monument West

3a Lafayette Park, the White House, & the Ellipse

Map locating most of the statues and monuments discussed in this section of the guide. *Map courtesy of the National Park Service, U.S. Department of the Interior.*

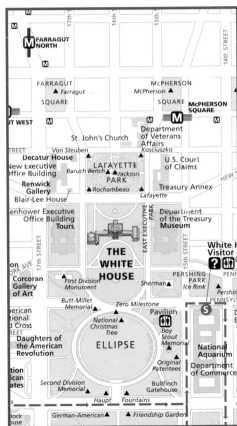

Albert Gallatin

Draped in a long coat, head cocked slightly to one side, his left hand resting on his hip, Albert Gallatin looks almost imperious, patently proud of his condensed credentials inscribed on the granite pedestal beneath him:

ALBERT GALLATIN/SECRETARY OF THE TREASURY/ GENIUS OF FINANCE/SENATOR AND REPRESENTA-TIVE/COMMISSIONER FOR THE TREATY OF GHENT/ MINISTER TO FRANCE AND GREAT BRITAIN/AND STEADFAST CHAMPION OF DEMOCRACY/1761-1849.

The eight-foot bronze statue of the fourth Secretary of the Treasury is one of many sculptures in the portfolio of the great James Earle Fraser. The dedication of the Gallatin statue came in October of 1947, after a two-decade process marred by both partisan bickering and delays caused by the Second World War. Democrats long regarded Gallatin with the iconic stature with which Republicans held Alexander Hamilton. The Republicans in Congress grudgingly agreed to allow a portrait statue of Gallatin to be erected on the north patio, with the stipulation that no public funds be used (Goode: 370).

A Swiss national, Gallatin had a long and prominent career in American politics, serving as a senator, representative for Pennsylvania, and finally as Secretary of the Treasury to both Thomas Jefferson and James Madison. Gallatin served the longest term as Secretary of the Treasury to date, from 1801 until

Albert Gallatin, "genius of finance," stands before the steps of the north patio of the United States Treasury. *Photos courtesy of United States Department of the Treasury.*

1814. Two years after his resignation, President Madison tried to persuade Gallatin to return to his former post, but he declined. Gallatin was meticulous in his duties as Secretary of the Treasury, and held strict financial accountability and a balanced budget paramount. He once remarked, "... I am not wrong in the belief that [America's] public funds are more secure than those of all the European powers" (U.S. Treasury). During his five-year stint as a diplomat, he brokered the Treaty of Ghent in 1814, which officially ended the War of 1812. Like any politi-

cian, Gallatin was not without enemies, many of whom cited his foreign birth as a basis for questioning his citizenship. His greatest rival was Alexander Hamilton, whose statue is perhaps appropriately situated on the Treasury Building's South Patio, so that even in posterity, the two need not associate.

Location: North patio of the Treasury Building, E and 15th streets, N.W.

Alexander Hamilton

The memorial for the first Secretary of the Treasury is appropriately located in front of the Treasury Building, at E and 15th streets. Clad in his finest livery, as he was wonted, Alexander Hamilton stands with a noble, slightly imperious pose atop his granite pedestal. The long, flowing cape in which he is draped gives him an almost regal air.

The inscription on the base of the statue reads:

ALEXANDER HAMILTON/1757-1804/FIRST SECRETARY OF THE TREASURY/SOLDIER ORATOR STATESMAN/CHAMPION OF CONSTITUTIONAL UNION/REPRESENTATIVE GOVERNMENT AND/NATIONAL INTEGRITY.

The inscription is bordered by bas-relief Roman fasces on either side.

President Warren G. Harding spoke at the 1923 dedication. An anonymous donor paid for the statue.

Hamilton was an accomplished businessman and politician. Among his many legacies were the Bank of New York, established in 1788, and the *New York Post*, which he founded in 1801. After representing New York at the Continental Congress in 1787, Hamilton co-authored a series of essays known as *The Federalist Papers*, in which he urged New Yorkers to ratify the Constitution. As Secretary of the Treasury, he clashed frequently with Secretary of State Thomas Jefferson, an anti-Federalist who championed individual states' rights over a strong central government. Hamilton's tax on whiskey sparked a rebellion by Pennsylvania farmers, which was quelled without bloodshed when George Washington dispatched a huge military force. As Hamilton put it, "A large army has cooled the courage of these madmen ..." (Keller:56).

Alexander Hamilton, the first Secretary of the Treasury. *Photo courtesy of United States Department of the Treasury.*

On July 11, 1804, Hamilton was mortally wounded in a duel with long-time rival Aaron Burr, who had been Jefferson's vice president. By killing Hamilton, Burr had committed political suicide. He was excoriated by an outraged American public, and narrowly escaped a murder conviction. Ironically, Hamilton's oldest son, Philip, had been killed in a duel three years earlier.

Location: South Patio of the Treasury Building, E and 15th streets.

Andrew Jackson

Much has been made of the fact that when Clark Mills created the dynamic sculpture of Major General Andrew Jackson on a rearing mount, he had never before seen an equestrian statue. Mills experimented with several models before perfecting his design, and solved an architectural dilemma that had stymied many other artists. Despite the steed's unwieldy position, the entire piece is perfectly balanced, a testament to the sculptor's ingenuity (Craven: 170). For over 150 years, Jackson has stood in the center of the seven-acre park between H Street and Pennsylvania Avenue N.W., surrounded by generals Lafayette, Von Steuben, Rochambeau, and Kosciuszko. Jackson is the only American and the only non-Revolutionary War general represented in Lafayette Park. Horse and rider are depicted in the moments before Jackson's victory over the British at the Battle of New Orleans. Jackson is tipping his hat to his troops, returning their salutes. In terms of military significance, the battle was pointless, as a truce had already been signed. But the victory was a huge morale boost for the United States, and elevated "Old Hickory" to iconic status.

The statue was cast from bronze cannons seized by Jackson during the War of 1812, and rests on a granite pedestal which is inscribed with Jackson's name, and the words "The Federal Union, It Must Be Preserved." The statue was assembled from ten separate pieces. Surrounding the base are four cannons that Jackson captured from Spanish forces fighting for control of Florida. An iron fence borders the grassy perimeter.

The Jackson memorial is the oldest surviving equestrian statue in the United States. An earlier equestrian statue in New York of King George III was melted down to make bullets during the Revolutionary War.

An auspicious chance meeting with the chairman of the Jackson Memorial Committee landed Mills the $32,000 commission. Upon conversing with Mills and learning that he was a sculptor, the chairman persuaded him to submit a design (ibid).

Thousands flocked to the dedication ceremonies, held on January 8, 1853, the thirty-eighth anniversary of the Battle of New Orleans. Among those in attendance were President Franklin Pierce and his cabinet, the Supreme Court justices, members of the House and Senate, and numerous retired army and navy officers. Senator Stephen A. Douglas of Illinois delivered the keynote speech just before the unveiling.

A native of South Carolina, Andrew Jackson served briefly as a representative and then Senator for Tennessee, where he had lived and practiced law as a young man. He narrowly lost the 1824 presidential election to John Adams, but defeated his former nemesis four years later, going on to serve two terms.

Possessed of a fiery temper, Jackson had killed a man in a duel for slandering his wife, Rachel. Rachel never wanted her husband to become president, as she was tired of the harrying pace of political life. She died three years after Jackson took office. Jackson followed in 1845, at the age of seventy-eight, and was buried at the Hermitage, his home in Nashville, Tennessee.

Location: Between H Street and Pennsylvania Avenue N.W., in Lafayette Park.

Major General Andrew Jackson, by Clark Mills, rears regally upon his steed in the center of Lafayette Park. *Photos by Maureen R. Quinn.*

Boy Scout Memorial

On November 7, 1964, the largest gathering of Boy Scouts since the organization's first National Jamboree twenty-seven years earlier converged on Washington, D.C.'s President's Park. Of little importance was the fact that the memorial that they were unveiling commemorated a milestone reached five years earlier. The great bronze statuary group by New York sculptor Donald Delue represented all Scouts past and present, as well as the noble ideals on which the Boy Scouts were founded over half a century ago. Referred to commonly as the Boy Scout Memorial, the sculpture's official name is the Commemorative Tribute. Among the dignitaries present at the dedication was Supreme Court justice Tom Clark, marking his fiftieth anniversary as an Eagle Scout.

A young Boy Scout is flanked by the allegorical figures of Mankind and Womankind, who embody the positive traits traditionally associated with their respective genders. The Boy Scout represents all Scouts, in the United States and abroad. The figures are larger than life – the Boy Scout is seven feet tall, and the man and woman are twelve and eleven feet, respectively. There is a thirty-foot by forty-foot pool, eighteen inches deep, next to the sculpture, and the Boy Scout oath is inscribed on a six-foot granite pedestal:

The Boy Scout Memorial, dedicated in 1964 to commemorate a half-century of scouting. *Photo courtesy of Boy Scouts of America National Council.*

On my honor, I will do my best/To do my duty to God and my country and to obey the Scout Law/To help other people at all times/To keep myself physically strong, mentally awake, and morally straight.

Architect William Henry Deacy, also of New York City, worked with Delue on the project. Deacy designed the National Science Gold Medal, given annually by the President of the United States to individuals who have contributed most to the advancement of science.

In 1959, Congress passed a bill setting aside public land in the District of Columbia for the erection of a Boy Scout memorial. Although the land was appropriated by the government, the memorial was funded with private donations. In soliciting contributions, the national headquarters of the Boys Scouts of America mailed cards with fifty dime-sized slots to the respective Boy Scout units across the nation. The number of slots represented the years that the Boy Scouts had been in existence. Donors were also asked to sign tiny scrolls, which were eventually placed inside the pedestal of the memorial.

Location: 15th Street NW, between E Street and Constitution Avenue, in President's Park.

David G. Farragut

A ten-foot bronze statue of David Glasgow Farragut – the first person to hold the rank of full admiral in the United States Navy – stands atop a twenty-foot granite pedestal on a small, grassy mound surrounded by an iron fence. The admiral is holding a telescope in both hands, and his right foot is resting on a wooden pier post. Farragut is attired in full uniform, with his long coat and cap, and a sword in a scabbard hanging at his side. Inscribed on the pedestal, directly underneath the statue, is "FARRAGUT." Around the base of the monument are four naval cannons. Both the statue and the cannons were cast from the propellers of Farragut's flagship, the U.S.S. *Hartford*.

In 1874, the Joint Committee on Public Buildings and Grounds selected twenty-six-year-old Vinnie Ream to create the memorial to the late admiral. Nine years earlier, Ream became the first woman to secure a commission for a public work of art, a statue of Abraham Lincoln in the Capital Rotunda. This was remarkable for a girl of fifteen. She received $20,000 for the Farragut Monument.

Born in Tennessee in 1801, Farragut was a lifelong sailor, enlisting in the navy as a midshipman at the age of nine, and serving aboard the U.S.S. *Essex* under Commodore David Porter during the War of 1812. Appointed flag officer of the West Gulf Blockading Squadron during the Civil War, Farragut won considerable acclaim with his capture of New Orleans in 1862. His decision to fight for the Union, however, led to tension between him and his relatives.

August of 1864 found Farragut leading a fleet into Mobile Bay, off of the coast of Alabama. He had ordered his officers to sail around a floating minefield, the edge of which was marked with black buoys. Most of the "torpedoes" were duds, although one of the ships in Farragut's fleet, the *Tecumseh*, had struck one earlier and sunk, resulting in the deaths of Commodore Tunis Craven and nearly 100 sailors. Fearing that his ship would be next, the captain of the *Brooklyn* had stopped his vessel. Not wanting to waste time, Farragut decided to simply sail around *Brooklyn*, and have the rest of the fleet follow. Passing to the port side of the stalled *Brooklyn*, Farragut's fleet captain Percival Drayton asked *Brooklyn's* captain what the problem was. "Torpedoes," came the reply, to which Farragut shouted, "Damn the torpedoes! Full speed ahead, Drayton!" (Hearn: 263).

Location: Farragut Square, 17th and K streets N.W.

Sculptor Vinnie Ream received $20,000 for the memorial to David G. Farragut, the U.S. Navy's first full admiral. *Photo courtesy of Bull Run Civil War Round Table.*

First Division Monument

On October 4, 1924, when Daniel R. Edwards pulled the cords that drew back the flags covering the granite and bronze memorial, he probably thought of his fellow soldiers of the First Infantry Division who made the ultimate sacrifice during the World War. He may also have thought how lucky he was that his name was not one of the 5,516 on the memorial bronze plaque on the front of the white granite pedestal. Six years earlier, while serving in France with Company C of the Third Machine Gun Battalion, the twenty-one-year-old private had crawled into a trench occupied by eight German soldiers, half of whom he killed, and half of whom he captured. At the time, Edwards had a broken arm. While he was returning to camp with the captured enemy soldiers, a mortar explosion killed one of the prisoners and seriously injured Edwards (U.S. Army). For his actions that July day, Edwards received the Congressional Medal of Honor.

The inevitability of future conflicts has necessitated that some monuments be works in progress. Over the years, additions commemorating the First Division dead from subsequent wars have added nearly 8,000 more names and cost approximately $220,000. These additions consist of bronze panels mounted on granite blocks, which surround the base of the main memorial. The first such addition, in honor of World War II dead, was installed in 1957, and designed by architect Cass Gilbert, Jr., whose father had designed the original monument. Twenty years later, the Vietnam addition was placed on the opposite side, and in 1995, one for Operation Desert Storm was added. The latter two were both designed by a team of architects from Philadelphia.

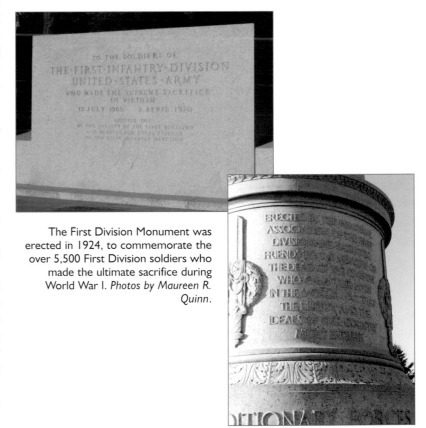

The First Division Monument was erected in 1924, to commemorate the over 5,500 First Division soldiers who made the ultimate sacrifice during World War I. *Photos by Maureen R. Quinn.*

The original First Division Monument consists of the afore-mentioned white granite pedestal, thirty feet in height, on top of which rises a thirty-five-foot pink granite shaft. Crowning the latter is a fifteen-foot gilded bronze statue of Victory, sculpted by Daniel Chester French. French, whose credits include the Lincoln Memorial, the Rear Admiral Samuel Francis Dupont Memorial Fountain, and the Thomas Hopkins Gallaudet Memorial, was an outstanding artist who served as chairman of the Commission of Fine Arts from 1912 to 1915. President William Howard Taft once called French "the greatest of living American sculptors" (Reps: 258).

The Society of the First Division raised the original monument at a cost of $115,000. Major General Charles P. Summerall, who was president of the society, wanted a monument similar to the Battle Monument at West Point, which commemorates 2,230 soldiers of the United States Regular Army killed during the Civil War. The dedication ceremony for the First Division Monument in 1924 came on the heels of a great parade. Among those in attendance at the unveiling was President Calvin Coolidge.

Location: State Place and 17ᵗʰ Street, west of the White House and south of the Eisenhower Building, in President's Park.

The thirty-foot white granite pillar is crowned by a fifteen-foot gilded statue of Victory, which was sculpted by Daniel Chester French. *Photos by Maureen R. Quinn.*

Friedrich Wilhelm von Steuben

In 1910, Major General Friedrich Wilhelm von Steuben (1730-1794) took his place in Lafayette Park among his four fellow generals – his contemporaries, Lafayette, Rochambeau, and Kosciusko – and the possibly misplaced but irreplaceable Andrew Jackson. Von Steuben's memorial was the last erected in the seven-acre park, completing the distinguished quorum that has gazed down upon visitors for nearly a century. Created by New York sculptor Albert Jaegers, the eight-foot heroic bronze features the stout, portly general in his officer's uniform, as imposing in posterity as he was in life. Beneath a bas-relief eagle on the front of the pedestal is a very lengthy inscription, affixed with bronze letters onto the granite. Shorter, ancillary pedestals flanking the main one bear allegorical sculptures. At the general's lower right, a soldier wearing only a helmet and sandals is seated on a bench, next to a naked young man holding a drawn sword. The inscription below them reads "MILITARY INSTRUCTION." Opposite them, "COMMEMORATION" shows a woman seated on a bench next to a tree, while a child kneels before her. Congress appropriated $50,000 for the memorial, and an additional $2,500 for the dedication.

Ironically, German-American relations were to collapse in less than a decade following the December 7 unveiling of the von Steuben statue, with the interception by British intelligence of the so-called Zimmermann Telegram, which urged Mexico to make war upon her northern neighbor. But no one at the dedication ceremony that day could ever have guessed at that, as American and German diplomats and dignitaries sat side-by-side, and a huge military parade followed the unveiling. President William Howard Taft gave local government employees the day off, and thousands of members of German-American societies thronged into the capital for the ceremony and accompanying festivities. Attendees from both sides of the Atlantic joined in song and revelry, and the ensuing celebrations eclipsed the actual unveiling. The Washington Post reported that hotels in the District were so full that some guests were lodged in the hotels' parlors. Taft's daughter, Helen, unveiled the statue, and a thunderous thirteen-gun artillery salute followed.

Von Steuben had been a captain in Frederick the Great's army. He had the good fortune to meet Benjamin Franklin in France in 1777, and Franklin wrote a glowing letter of recommendation to George Washington. This coupled with the endorsement of the French minister of war secured a position for Von Steuben in the American Army. An affable but strict taskmaster, Von Steuben instilled much-needed discipline into Washington's ragtag troops at Valley Forge in 1778, turning them into a bona fide fighting force in record time. This feat was even more impressive given the fact that Von Steuben spoke no English when he first arrived, and relied on several aides-de-camp to translate his orders to the men. When he lost his temper, Von Steuben swore at the soldiers in German. Soon realizing the limited effectiveness of this tactic, he translated the profanities into French for Captain Benjamin Walker, who in turn cursed at the troops in English for him (Independence Hall Association)!

Von Steuben's initial motivation for helping the Americans was monetary. After his stint in the Prussian army he experienced financial hardship, and unsuccessfully sought appointments with foreign armies. He was finally rewarded with a $2,500 annual pension in 1790, and a 16,000-acre estate in New York (ibid). After the war, Von Steuben was declared a United States citizen.

Location: Jackson Place and H Street, in Lafayette Park.

Baron Friedrich Wilhelm von Steuben was the last general to take his place among the other military heroes immortalized in Lafayette Park. *Photo by Maureen R. Quinn.*

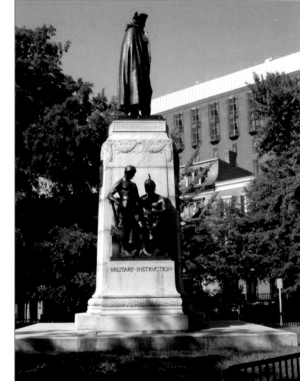

The sculpture group "Military Instruction" depicts a soldier teaching a young man how to wield a sword. *Photo by Maureen R. Quinn.*

Gilbert de Lafayette

Since 1853, Major General Andrew Jackson and his rearing mount held dominion in the rectangular plot of ground located south of H Street and north of Pennsylvania Avenue. Although the park had been re-named Lafayette Square during the French nobleman's final visit to the United States in 1824, nearly seventy more years would pass before Lafayette would be honored with his own monument. In 1855, Congress appropriated $50,000 for the Lafayette memorial. That memorial was finally erected without ceremony in April of 1891.

An eight-and-a-half-foot bronze likeness of Gilbert de Lafayette (1757-1834) surmounts an ornately-carved marble pedestal approximately twenty-five feet in height, and surrounded by seven additional bronze sculptures at its base. The intent of sculptors Jean Falquière and Marius Mercié was to depict Lafayette petitioning the French National Assembly in 1778 for military assistance to the struggling thirteen Colonies. Contemporaries of Lafayette, among them Rochambeau, flank both sides of the pedestal. In the front, stretching her arm forth to hand the marquis a sword, is a half-naked woman representing America. On the opposite side are two cherubs. An inscription below Lafayette, in the center of the pedestal, reads "To General Lafayette and his Compatriots, 1777-1783." Directly above the two cherubs is "By the Congress, in commemoration of the services rendered by General Lafayette and his compatriots during the struggle for the independence of the United States of America." Lafayette's was the second of five monuments erected in the park that bears his name.

The assistance of several European powers, principally France, contributed significantly to an eventual American victory in the Revolutionary War. But underneath the ostensible altruistic motivations was probably a desire for revenge on the part of the French, who had lost their Canadian possessions to England in the Seven Years' War (1756-1763). The French must have been only too glad to return the favor when the opportunity presented itself.

The original plan called for the Lafayette memorial to be placed several yards to the west of the current spot, midway between Jackson Place and Madison Place. This was scuttled when critics pointed out that the location would block the view of the Jackson statue. The pedestal, which had already been placed accordingly, was subsequently moved (Goode: 373).

In 1776, a nineteen-year-old Lafayette set sail for America. Among those traveling with him was a young engineer named Pierre Charles L'Enfant. The best known of the foreign military leaders who assisted the colonies during the revolution, Lafayette had been a captain in the French army. Upon arriving in America, he was made a major general in the Continental Army, where he served alongside George Washington in several campaigns. The two developed a deep mutual respect and affection for one another.

Ten years before his death, Lafayette made a final visit to America, accompanied by his son. They visited every state, and observed first hand that the love and admiration of a grateful country had not diminished at all in the thirty-one years since the end of the American Revolution.

Location: Pennsylvania Avenue and 16th Street, in Lafayette Park.

Gilbert de Lafayette and his bronze entourage, sculpted by Jean Falquière and Marius Mercié. *Photo by Maureen R. Quinn.*

At the base of the Lafayette monuments, Lady America stretches forth her arm to hand the marquis a sword. *Photo by Maureen R. Quinn.*

James B. McPherson

Statues spark a thousand questions in the minds of viewers, the more elaborate or exaggerated the subject's pose, the more inquisitive the viewer's mind waxes. Those passing by the bronze equestrian statue of Major General James Birdseye McPherson might wonder at the curious stance of his horse – right front hoof raised in the air, mouth open in a silent snort. Is the animal alarmed, about to rear up on its hind legs from some shock? McPherson, calmer yet quite alert, clutches the reins loosely in his left hand, while he holds a pair of binoculars in his right. His gaze appears locked on something that he has either just observed, or is preparing to inspect. Those familiar with Civil War history might surmise that the general is depicted in his fatal encounter with stray Confederate troops at the Battle of Atlanta on July 22, 1864. Recognizing McPherson, a band of rebel soldiers in the woods near Atlanta demanded that he surrender at once. When he instead turned his horse around and attempted to flee, they opened fire. McPherson's date of death is inscribed on one side of the sculpture's base, and opposite, "ERECTED BY HIS COMRADES/OF THE SOCIETY OF/THE ARMY OF THE TENNESSEE." At the time of his death, McPherson had recently replaced William Tecumseh Sherman as commander of the Army of the Tennessee.

The memorial was created by sculptor Louis Rebisso. Bucking the trend for the time – an American artist working from his European studio – Rebisso was an Italian expatriate living in Cincinnati. He received about $50,000 for this commission, half of the funds being appropriated by Congress. Confederate cannons seized at the Battle of Atlanta were melted down to cast this statue.

The Society of the Army of the Tennessee wanted Rebisso's sculpture to be more than just a memorial to their fallen comrade; they had planned to have McPherson's remains exhumed from a cemetery in his hometown in Clyde, Ohio and re-interred in a vault that would form the base of the equestrian statue, but this was not feasible.

Location: H and 15th streets.

Jean de Rochambeau

The fact that there are two statues of Major General Comte Jean de Rochambeau (1725-1807) in Washington, D.C. has not saved him from the almost inevitable curse of oblivion that befalls so many historical figures. While most Americans have heard of Gilbert de Lafayette, they are unfamiliar with Rochambeau, who came to their shores in 1780 with a force of 5,500 French troops, and fought alongside George Washington at Yorktown. The first statue of the French count is located on the west side of the pedestal of Lafayette's monument, next to the Chevalier Duportail, who has also suffered posthumous anonymity. The second statue is an eight-foot heroic bronze that is supposed to be the central figure in the monument to Rochambeau himself. Rochambeau is depicted leading his troops against the British during the American Revolution. His right hand is presumably pointed at the enemy, while his left hand clutches his battle plans. His name is inscribed below him.

Privately, Rochambeau had serious misgivings about the American forces, whom he deemed poorly-trained, ill-equipped, and unprepared. After arriving in Rhode Island, he drilled his own troops while awaiting reinforcements from France. He was unswayed by Lafayette's urging him to move more quickly against the British (PBS).

On a ledge near the base is a sculptural group much more dramatic, and one that, critics might argue, draws attention away from Rochambeau. Liberty, a majestic lady in long, flowing robes, has just disembarked from a ship in the background. In her left hand she holds the French and American flags, and in her right hand, a sword. Beside her is America, a feisty eagle straining to hold onto a shield dangling from his right claw. In bas-relief on the pedestal's sides are the coats-of-arms of France and Rochambeau. The inscription on the rear of the pedestal, the north side, is from a letter that Washington wrote to Rochambeau after the war. The sculptor was J.J. Fernand Hamar.

Rochambeau points toward the enemy, while clutching the battle plans in his other hand. On a ledge beneath him are Lady Liberty and America.
Photos by Maureen R. Quinn.

During the May 24, 1902 dedication there was no question as to who Rochambeau was, and stands were erected in Lafayette Park to accommodate the hundreds who turned out. As a symbol of the unity that had contributed to the victory in the Revolutionary War, the monument was draped in both the French and American flags, and a ceremonial guard of two French sailors and two American Marines stood at the corners. Diplomatic representatives from France, Germany, Italy, Russia, and China sat alongside President Theodore Roosevelt and his cabinet, along with military officers from several different countries. Roosevelt delivered a 400-word speech prior to the unveiling. The American ambassador to France and his French counterpart also addressed the crowd, amid bursts of patriotic euphony from a pair of military bands.

Location: Pennsylvania Avenue and Jackson Place, Lafayette Park.

John Barry

Perhaps his native country's own struggle with England was what drove Irishman John Barry (1745-1803) to take up arms against her so effectively during his adopted country's fight for independence. A versatile sailor, he smoothly made the transition from merchant mariner to naval officer to privateer, as the situation required. He had served as a captain in the Continental Navy, and was appointed to the same rank in the United States Navy, which he was instrumental in founding in 1794. In February of 1797, George Washington signed Barry's commission for the latter, and made it retroactive to 1794. Like his contemporaries John Paul Jones and Gustavus Conygham, Barry served his new nation with dedication and zeal, capturing numerous British vessels. Though victorious in most of his battles, Barry lost his thirty-two-gun ship *Raleigh* after an ambush by three British ships in September of 1778. He must have felt somewhat vindicated, however, when his ship *Alliance* soundly defeated the twenty-eight-gun British *Sybylle* five years later, during the final naval battle of the Revolutionary War. Throughout his forty-three-year maritime career, Barry commanded no less than seven ships. The man who has been dubbed "the Father of the United States Navy" died at his Strawberry Hill estate in Philadelphia in 1803, at the age of fifty-eight.

An eight-foot bronze statue of Commodore Barry stands on an elaborate marble pedestal. Barry is attired in full naval uniform, and he is draped in a long cloak. His right hand rests on the hilt of his sheathed sword, which he holds in front of him like a walking stick. Beneath the commodore, on the front of the pedestal, stands a robed female figure upon the prow of a ship. She holds a laurel branch, representing victory, in one hand. On her right is an eagle. Barry's name is inscribed on a tablet directly below her. Sculptor John J. Boyle received $50,000 for the piece.

A huge military parade preceded the memorial's May 16, 1914 dedication. Speaking to the thousands in attendance, President Woodrow Wilson focused on the general theme of patriotism, and said that Barry, although foreign-born, was not an "Irish-American," but "an Irishman who became an American."

Location: I and 14th streets, in Franklin Park.

John J. Pershing/ American Expeditionary Forces (AEF) Memorial

The statue of General John J. "Black Jack" Pershing stands atop a granite pedestal at 14th Street and Pennsylvania Avenue, N.W., in the park that bears his name. Pershing's right hand is deferentially placed over his heart, and he is holding his hat with his left hand, as if he is reciting the Pledge of Allegiance. Inscribed on the base of the pedestal are the dates of his life, 1860-1948. Pershing was in charge of the American Expeditionary Forces (AEF) during World War I. About two million soldiers were under his command. He was eventually given the title "General of the Armies." Pershing Park was dedicated in 1981, and the general's statue was added in 1983.

Pershing graduated from West Point in 1886, and later earned his law degree from the University of Nebraska. He served during the Spanish-American War, notably at the battle of San Juan

Hill as a cavalry lieutenant (Lawson: 22). He suffered a devastating tragedy in 1912 when his wife, Frances, and three daughters perished in a fire at the Presidio, a military post in San Francisco. Only his son, Warren, survived. Pershing was away at the time.

Prior to his service during World War I, Pershing was placed in charge of a unit that was sent to Mexico to capture Pancho Villa, whose raid on a Mexican village had resulted in the deaths of several American citizens.

Pershing pursued the infamous bandit and revolutionary, but never caught him. Later that same year, on July 4, 1917, Pershing arrived at the tomb of Lafayette in Paris and supposedly proclaimed, "Lafayette, we are here!" Pershing died in 1948 at the age of eighty-seven, and was buried in Arlington National Cemetery.

Location: 14th Street and Pennsylvania Avenue, N.W.

John J. "Black Jack" Pershing, General of the Armies, commander of the AEF during the First World War. *Photos by Maureen R. Quinn.*

Second Division Memorial

Major General James G. Harbord directed his remarks to the 3,000 men who had served under his command eighteen years ago to the day, when as young soldiers they had repulsed the German advance on Paris in the final year of the First World War. The Second Infantry Division veterans, Harbord recalled, had withstood the enemy assault at the battles of Château-Thierry and Belleau Woods in France. At the end of the Great War, Second Division casualties numbered 25,000, including 4,500 killed. In the two major wars to follow, the death toll for the division would rise to nearly 18,000.

In a show of camaraderie with his former troops, the aging commander reminisced about "weary days of billets and battle; of crashing night when the skies split red, of long gray miles in the rain" (*New York Times*).

Also attending the July 18, 1936 dedication were "the Gold Star Mothers," who had lost sons in the First World War. As part of the ceremony, one of the women laid a wreath at the base of the memorial.

In the center of a huge granite façade is an eighteen-foot gilded bronze hand brandishing a flaming sword, symbolically blocking the German advance into Paris. Inscribed on either side of the blade are the names of the twelve World War I battles in which the Second Division fought. Sculptor James Earle Fraser and architect John Russell Pope collaborated on this touching tribute, whose $60,000 cost was borne by the Society of the Second Division. Construction of the memorial had been approved in 1931 by a joint resolution of Congress. In 1962, wings were added to the memorial, to commemorate Second Division veterans who lost their lives in World War II and the Korean War.

The centerpiece of the Second Division Memorial is an eighteen-foot gilded bronze hand brandishing a flaming sword, symbolically blocking the German advance into Paris during World War I. *Photo by Maureen R. Quinn.*

Even as Harbord addressed the crowd with somber, yet celebratory recollections, that which remained unsaid was likely on everyone's mind: that powerful, sinister forces were once again on the move in Europe, and that the Second Division might soon be called upon to do what they had done so valiantly a generation ago. But this time, the Allies would be too late to prevent the fall of the French capital, and the ensuing carnage over six years would dwarf that of the earlier conflict.

Location: Constitution Avenue and 17th Street, N.W.

Settlers of the District of Columbia Memorial

Sculpted by Carl Mose and dedicated April 25, 1936, this granite monument consists of a simple rectangular shaft upon a pedestal. On each of the shaft's four sides is a one-foot square bas relief carving depicting an agricultural subject. Inscribed around the memorial's base are the names of the eighteen landowners whose properties were acquired and consolidated to create the nation's capital. Another inscription reads, in part: ". . .to the original patentees prior to 1700 whose land grants embrace the site of the federal city." The memorial was erected by the National Society of the Daughters of the American Colonists.

The sculptor had been an instructor at the Corcoran Gallery of Art (Marine Corps Marathon).

Location: E and 15th streets.

Thaddeus Kosciuszko

Thaddeus Kosciuszko's memorial in Lafayette Park is misleading, giving the impression that he was killed in battle. The greatest "evidence" for this erroneous conclusion are the two bronze figures on the western side of the base. A reclining Kosciuszko, apparently mortally wounded, is pointing toward the battlefield and urging the Polish soldier standing next to him to return to the fight. Eagles atop quarter hemispheres are replicated on the front and rear of the base, to show Kosciuszko's close connection with both his native and adopted countries. But underneath the eagle sculpture at the rear is the inscription "RACLAWICE," referring to the site of Kosciuszko's defeat by Czarist forces in 1794. An inscription above that, on the granite pedestal, reads "And freedom shrieked as Kosciuszko fell." Kosciuszko did not die at Raclawice, but was captured and imprisoned for two years, after which he was exiled. He died in Switzerland in 1817, at the age of seventy-one, and his body was returned to Poland for burial.

The eight-foot heroic bronze in the center shows Kosciusko in a patient pose, arms resting at his sides, holding in his right hand a furled piece of paper which contains his plans for the fortifications of the American fort at Saratoga. Underneath him is his name. The eastern side of the base, opposite Kosciuszko and the Polish soldier, shows Brigadier General Kosciuszko untying the bound hands of an American soldier. The sculptor for the monument was Antoni Popiel.

In February 1910, Congress appropriated $3,500 for site preparation for the dedication, which began at 4:00 p.m. on May 11, and followed an earlier unveiling of the Casimir Pulaski statue at Pennsylvania Avenue and 13th Street. Attending were members of the Polish National Alliance, various Polish-American organizations throughout the country, as well as dignitaries from Poland, Germany, Austria, and Belgium.

Some of the thousands who packed into Lafayette Park for the ceremony must have flinched when Secretary of War Jacob M. Dickinson, in accepting the statue on behalf of the United States, referred to Poland as "that unhappy land symbolizing in story and in song all that is most gallant and most pathetic in the histories of the nations." He was, however, merely comparing the two countries' respective struggles for freedom, only one of which was successful.

Thousands of Polish-Americans attended the May 11, 1910 dedication ceremony for the memorial to Brigadier General Thaddeus Kosciuszko. *Photos by Maureen R. Quinn.*

In addition to his skill as a military commander, Kosciuszko was a superb engineer whose solid fortifications helped cement the American defenses. He was a good friend of Thomas Jefferson, who called him "the purest son of liberty." Although Kosciuszko was made an American citizen by a grateful Continental Congress following the Revolutionary War and given a 500-acre estate in Ohio, he never forgot his roots, returning to Poland a year after the Treaty of Paris to secure for his homeland what he had helped secure for America. He vowed "I swear to the whole Polish nation that I shall not use the power vested in me for private oppression but that I shall exercise this power only in the defense of the whole of the frontiers and to regain the independence of the [n]ation and to establish universal freedom" (PolskiInternet.com).

Location: H Street and Madison Place, in Lafayette Park.

William Tecumseh Sherman

In 1895, the William T. Sherman Memorial Commission's selection of a design by Carl Rohl-Smith was received with discord among the press and the artistic community. Several members of The National Sculpture Society, who had served the commission in an advisory capacity, had regarded Rohl-Smith's design as inferior. Ironically, after enduring the "slings and arrows" of petulant journalists and envious colleagues, Rohl-Smith died suddenly in 1897, while visiting his native Denmark. His widow, Sara, supervised completion of the memorial. Erected by the Society of the Army of the Tennessee, the elaborate monument cost nearly $150,000, the bulk of which was borne by the government (Jacob: 93-95).

Incorporating both historical and Classical elements, the Sherman Memorial astounds viewers with its detail and complexity. Steps on all four sides lead to a granite platform, whose corners are guarded by bronze soldiers representing the artillery, cavalry, engineers, and infantry. In the center is an immense pedestal, capped with the bronze figure of General Sherman astride his horse. Together, horse and rider stand fourteen feet tall. Inscribed around the base are the names of Sherman's thirty-five battles, among them the Capture of Atlanta. Allegorical figures dramatically depicting both War and Peace stand on the opposite sides of the pedestal, above bronze bas-relief panels flanked by portrait medallions of Union generals. Peace is depicted as a woman holding the traditional olive branch. Three children stand with her, one of whom is feeding a dove. War is fiercely rending her garments as she stands over the body of a soldier. Two vultures at her feet are preparing to devour the corpse. Panels on the front and back of the pedestal depict the capture of Atlanta. The monument is located at the spot where the proud general watched his men march down Pennsylvania Avenue in the grand review of Union troops following the war, in May of 1865.

Standard protocol at unveilings called for the monument to be draped on either side by an American flag, which was supported by a pair of ropes. On cue, a dignitary or someone with a special connection to the subject of the monument pulled a cord which drew the flags back, exposing the newly-dedicated monument for all to see. At the 1903 unveiling of the Sherman Memorial, this honor was given to his grandson, William Tecumseh Sherman Thorndike. President Theodore Roosevelt was also in attendance.

An 1840 West Point graduate, Sherman was given command of the Army of the Tennessee in 1863. He firmly believed that the best way to end a war quickly was to make the conflict as miserable as possible for the enemy, and he did just that. Hated in the South for the swath of death and destruction that he cut on his March to the Sea in 1865, Sherman was generally respected by Northerners, and immensely popular with his soldiers, who referred to him as "Uncle Billy." For members of the press, however, Sherman had little tolerance. After being liberated from their southern masters, thousands of slaves tagged along with Sherman's army, viewing the Union commander as an almost messianic figure. Friends and supporters begged him to run for president, but Sherman staunchly refused. He died in 1891.

Location: E and 15th streets, by the White House.

This grandiose monument to General William Tecumseh Sherman was erected in 1897 by the Society of the Army of the Tennessee, with the government's footing most of the $150,000 cost. *Photo courtesy of Bull Run Civil War Round Table.*

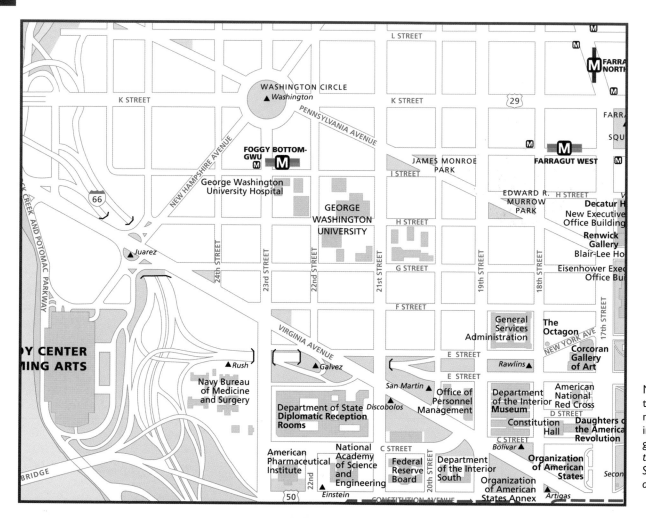

Map locating most of the statues and monuments discussed in this section of the guide. *Map courtesy of the National Park Service, U.S. Department of the Interior.*

3b From the White House to the Kennedy Center

Albert Einstein

Located on the grounds of the National Academy of Sciences (NAS), this twelve-foot, 7,000-pound statue depicts the pensive scientist reclining on three ascending, semi-circular white granite benches. Children are fond of sitting in Einstein's lap to pose for photographs. Created by New York sculptor Robert Berks, this immense bronze figure was welded together from nineteen separate sections, over a ten-month period. Among Berks' other projects are the figures for the Mary McLeod Bethune Memorial in Lincoln Park, and the bronze bust of John F. Kennedy at the Kennedy Center for the Performing Arts. In his left hand, Einstein clutches a sheet of paper containing notes and mathematical equations dealing with several of his theories, including that of relativity. At the German physicist's feet is a twenty-eight-foot diameter black granite map of the universe, set with 2,700 metal studs representing the various heavenly bodies exactly as they appeared in the night sky on the memorial's dedication date. The celestial map was diagrammed by two astronomers from the U.S. Naval Observatory, P. Kenneth Seidelman and Richard E. Schmidt. Architect James A. Van Sweden designed the landscaping. The memorial was unveiled April 22, 1979 at the annual meeting of the NAS.

The three quotations from Einstein that are inscribed on the center bench do not address abstruse mathematical formulas. They are plain, simple sentiments that appeal to the humanity in everyone.

As long as I have any choice in the matter, I shall live only in a country where civil liberty, tolerance, and equality of all citizens before the law prevail.

The rising tide of anti-Semitism convinced Einstein to flee Germany in 1933, when the Nazis came to power. He became an American citizen in 1940.

Joy and amazement of the beauty and grandeur of this world of which man can just form a faint notion.

The right to search for truth implies also a duty; one must not conceal any part of what one has recognized to be true.

In creating the giant bronze Einstein, Berks extrapolated from a bust that he had sculpted while visiting the late scientist at his Princeton, New Jersey, study in 1953. Einstein doubtless would have approved of the selection of Berks to again render him in bronze, as a 1954 letter that Einstein wrote indicates his approbation of Berks's original sculpture.

Einstein is considered by many to be the greatest scientist of all time. His 1916 publication "The Foundation of the General Theory of Relativity" explained the relationship between matter and energy, and is notated by the equation $E=mc^2$. In 1921, Einstein received the Nobel Prize in physics for his research on photo electricity – the process by which light particles striking metal cause the release of electrons (NAS). He became a full member of the NAS in 1942. Einstein died in 1955, at the age of seventy-six, in the midst of ongoing research.

Location: Constitution Avenue and 3rd Street, on the grounds of the National Academy of Sciences, in Potomac Park.

A pensive Albert Einstein, rendered in bronze by Robert Berks, ponders the mysteries of the universe.
Photos courtesy of National Academy of Sciences.

Alexander Pushkin

In his poem "Death Be Not Proud," seventeenth-century English writer John Donne notes, "The best men first with thee do go ...," and this was sadly the case with Russia's premiere poet, slain in a duel at age thirty-seven. Enraged to discover that his brother-in-law was secretly courting Pushkin's wife, Natalie, Pushkin provoked the former into challenging him to a duel. Both men were injured in the January 29, 1837, confrontation, Pushkin fatally. He died two days later.

Alexander (Aleksandr) S. Pushkin – a swarthy man with thick, dark curls and long sideburns – was very prolific during his short lifetime. In addition to his obvious poetic talents, he was also a playwright and author. His most notable work is arguably the novel *Eugene Onegin*, which he completed in 1831 after eight years. His literary career was not without controversy, and as a young man he was exiled for four years by the Czarist regime. A museum dedicated to the Muscovite writer is located in the Russian city that was renamed in his honor in 1937.

Father and son sculptors Alexander and Igor Bourganov resurrected Pushkin in a bronze sculpture, which stands proudly at H and 20th streets, on the grounds of George Washington University. Atop a column behind the statue of Pushkin is a golden Pegasus, which Alexander Bourganov explained was symbolic of the collaboration between Russia and the United States in the coming millennium (Berry). In 1998, representatives from the New York-based American-Russian Cultural Cooperation Foundation contacted GWU President Stephen J.

Trachtenberg about erecting a monument to Pushkin on the school's campus. Former Missouri congressman James W. Symington, who also chaired the foundation, noted that this would be the first time that a Russian was honored with a memorial in the United States.

Alexander Pushkin, Russia's premiere poet, memorialized in bronze on the grounds of George Washington University. *Photo courtesy of Julie Piraino-Woodford, George Washington University.*

The dedication was scheduled for June 6, 1999, the 200th anniversary of Pushkin's birth, but the statue had not been delivered yet. Nevertheless, a ceremony was held, with the actual unveiling's coming the following year. Among those in attendance at the September 20, 2000, unveiling were Deputy Secretary of State Strobe Talbott, Russian Foreign Minister Igor Ivanov, and Moscow's Mayor, Yuri Luzhkov, who presented the statue as a gift from the Russian capital to the city of Washington, D.C. The memorial plaque on the pedestal is an English translation of Pushkin's poem, "The Monument," and was translated by GWU professors Peter Rollberg and Jonathan Chaves (Rollberg). During the dedication ceremony, Rollberg read a translation of Pushkin's poem "To The Poet." The Pushkin memorial was funded through private contributions.

Location: H and 20th streets, on the campus of George Washington University.

Armenian Earthquake Memorial (Motherland)

On a late morning in December 1988, a 6.9 earthquake rumbled through a heavily-populated area in western Armenia, wreaking devastation in that Soviet bloc country, as well as in the adjacent republics of Azerbaijan and Georgia. Although the region was not unaccustomed to nature's vicissitudes, the inhabitants were caught flat-footed this time. Particularly hard hit were the Armenian cities of Spitak, Leninakan, and Kirovakan. Thousands were killed as buildings collapsed around them, leaving piles of rubble and twisted wreckage in their wake. Soviet Prime Minister Mikhail Gorbachev was visiting the United States when he was informed.

An eight-foot bronze woman clutching a child in her arms tells a silent tale of tragedy, courage, hope, and redemption. She and the little boy stare straight ahead, watching events unfold around them, safe for the moment but nonetheless apprehensive. Their facial features are well-defined, simultaneously portraying both resolve and trepidation. The lower half of the sculpture, especially the mother's dress, is more abstract, blending into the rock-shaped base beneath her. The inscription reads "To the American People from a grateful Armenian People – Earthquake Assistance, December 7, 1988." Known officially as "Motherland," the memorial is approximately fifteen feet high by seven feet wide by six feet long.

Attending the March 15, 1991 dedication were representatives from the Soviet Embassy, the American Red Cross, and the Armenian Assembly of America. With the fall of the Soviet Union in 1991, Armenia became independent.

American Red Cross President Elizabeth Dole – wife of Kansas senator Bob Dole – said at the dedication "Just as the child in this sculpture will forever remain in the embrace of its mother, so, too, will the people of Armenia forever remain in the heart of the Red Cross and in the heart of a good, caring, and generous nation" (American Red Cross).

Armenian sculptor Freidrich "Frid" Sogoyan created Motherland in his Moscow studio. Sogoyan was born in Leninakan, and said in an interview that he lost "thirty-two close friends in the 1988 earthquake." Sogoyan created many sculptures and monuments for the Soviet government, and he hinted during the same interview that much of his art might be considered communist propaganda by some. Sogoyan adapted well after the collapse of the Soviet state, finding many lucrative commissions from private individuals. He was hired by Gorbachev himself to create a graveyard memorial for the former Soviet premier's late wife, Raisa (Zenian).

Location: Red Cross Square, former American Red Cross headquarters, E and 17th streets, N.W.

Sculptor Friedrich Sogoyan's Motherland commemorates the assistance of the American people and the Red Cross in the aftermath of the 1988 Armenian Earthquake. *Photos courtesy of the American Red Cross. All rights reserved in all countries.*

Benito Juarez

Sculpted by Enrique Alciati and designed by architect Louis Ortiz Macedo, the twelve-foot bronze statue of Benito Juarez that stands at Virginia and New Hampshire avenues, N.W. was a reciprocal gift from Mexico in 1969, three years after the United States gave their southern neighbor a statue of Abraham Lincoln. Juarez's right hand symbolically points toward the bust of George Washington on the grounds of the university that bears the first U.S. President's name (Rosales and Jobe). The sculpture is a reproduction of the original located in Juarez's hometown of Guelatao, in the Mexican state of Oaxaca (wa-HA-ka).

Born to Zapotec Indian parents in 1806, Benito Juarez trekked to the state's capital in 1818, believing that he could make a better life for himself there. He earned a law degree, and was elected to the Oaxaca City Council, later to the state legislature, and eventually to two terms as governor. A contemporary who shared a mutual respect with Abraham Lincoln, Juarez was a tireless advocate of the poor and oppressed. His opposition to the tremendous power held by the Catholic Church and the aristocracy made him as many enemies as supporters. During his second term as governor, he helped draft Mexico's constitution, but its inherent political reforms angered many wealthy and powerful individuals, and Juarez was forced into a two-year exile in New Orleans. In 1861, he was elected president of Mexico, but the invasion of French troops a year later forced him and his cabinet to flee, roaming the countryside and rallying support wherever they could. In 1867, mounting pressure from the United States and the imminent Franco-Prussian War convinced Napoleon III to withdraw. Juarez was reinstated, and eventually elected to a second term. Exhausted and overworked, he died in 1872.

Location: Virginia and New Hampshire avenues, N.W.

Founders of the DAR (Daughters of the American Revolution) Memorial

The Daughters of the American Revolution (DAR) was founded in 1890 by Mary Lockwood Smith, Ellen Hardin Walworth, Mary Desha, and Eugenia Washington. Membership is open to any woman eighteen or older who can prove that she is a direct descendant of a Revolutionary War veteran. Sculptor Gertude Vanderbilt Whitney, who also created the *Titanic* Memorial, was a member of the DAR.

The marble memorial features a nine-foot cloaked female figure with open arms, standing on a three-tiered pedestal. The inscription on the low, horizontal wall behind her reads "TO THE WOMEN WHOSE PATRIOTIC FORESIGHT MADE POSSIBLE THE NATIONAL SOCIETY DAUGHTERS OF THE

AMERICAN REVOLUTION." On either side of the sculpture are two medallions, beneath which are inscribed the names, and dates of birth and death of the founders. The years are in Roman numerals. The medallions are reproductions of medals that the founders received in 1898.

Unveiled in 1929, this memorial by Gertrude Vanderbilt Whitney honors the four women who founded the Daughters of the American Revolution (DAR) in 1890 – Mary Lockwood Smith, Ellen Hardin Walworth, Mary Desha, and Eugenia Washington. *Photos courtesy National Society of the DAR.*

The dedication ceremony was held on April 17, 1929, the 154th anniversary of the Battle of Lexington and Concord, where the "shot heard 'round the world" was fired, marking the start of the American War of Independence.

Location: C and 18th streets, by DAR headquarters at 1776 D Street, N.W.

Jane A. Delano Memorial/ The Spirit of Nursing

The hands of the cloaked bronze figure are waist-level, her slightly-raised arms, splayed fingers, and upturned palms denoting a gesture of offering rather than supplication. She stands on a square pedestal, and seems to emerge from an alcove in the white marble stele directly behind her. On either side of the latter a curved bench extends, on which the inscription from the Ninety-first Psalm reassures visitors:

> Thou shalt not be afraid for the terror by night; nor for the arrow that flieth by day; nor for the pestilence that walketh in darkness; nor for the destruction that wasteth at noonday.

This tribute, called The Spirit of Nursing, was completed in 1933 and dedicated the following year. The memorial sits in a quiet courtyard formed by the three buildings that comprise Red Cross Square, site of the former headquarters of the American Red Cross.

The name of Jane A. Delano is unfamiliar to most laypersons, but her contributions to nursing were on par with those of Clara Barton and Florence Nightingale. Delano became superintendent of the Army Nurse Corps in 1909, resigning three years later to devote more time to her volunteer position as head of the Nursing Service of the American Red Cross, while also serving as president of the American Nurses' Association. Her death at a base hospital in France in April 1919 prompted thousands of nurses – both civilian and military – to petition for a memorial in her honor. Delano was buried in Arlington National Cemetery, in a section reserved for nurses.

Fourteen years elapsed before Philadelphia sculptor R. Tait McKenzie finally presented the finished piece to three members of the memorial committee. There had been considerable debate as to what form the memorial should take, and who exactly should be memorialized. The committee at last settled on a bronze and marble sculpture in a garden setting, and took a suggestion from a Pennsylvania senator to dedicate the memorial not only to Delano, but all of the 296 nurses who had lost their lives during the First World War.

The Jane A. Delano Memorial, also called The Spirit of Nursing, is dedicated to both her and the nearly 300 nurses who lost their lives during the First World War. *Photos courtesy of American Red Cross. All rights reserved in all countries.*

The dedication was held April 26, 1934, during the biennial convention of the three national nursing associations. Thousands of spectators jostled for position at the start of the ceremonies, many of them peering out the windows of the three surrounding Red Cross buildings. Anna Kerr, who had been a classmate of Delano's at Bellevue Hospital School of Nursing, and an original member of the memorial committee appointed in 1920, removed the banner with the Red Cross emblem that covered the bronze statue. Following the unveiling, five wreaths were laid at the base of the memorial, and the Marine Band's rendition of "Taps" floated wistfully into the air.

The guests that followed spoke reverently of Delano, as well as of the 20,000 nurses who served with her. During the war, half of those nurses were stationed overseas with the American Expeditionary Force, and former Surgeon General M. W. Ireland reminded the crowd that many nurses worked in field hospitals, where they were in nearly as much danger as troops on the front lines. For Mabel T. Boardman, Secretary of the American Red Cross, the memorial brought a verse from Exodus 3:5 to mind: ". . .put off thy shoes from thy feet, for the place whereon thou standest is holy ground."

Location: Red Cross Square, former American Red Cross headquarters, E and 17th streets, N.W.

John A. Rawlins

Sculptor Joseph A. Bailly's life-sized bronze statue of Major General John A. Rawlins depicts him in full military regalia, the Union insignia prominently displayed on both his belt buckle and hat. Rawlins is leaning on his sword, and in his right hand, he holds a pair of binoculars. The statue was erected in 1874. Between then and 1931, the Rawlins statue was moved three times, but eventually wound up back at its original location. Bailly was a forty-seven-year-old Parisian sculptor who was living in Philadelphia.

A close friend and advisor to General Ulysses S. Grant, Rawlins also served as Grant's Secretary of War from 1864 until Rawlins's death from tuberculosis in 1869. Born in Illinois in 1831, Rawlins was an attorney before the Civil War. He helped establish the 45th Illinois Infantry, at which time he met Grant (Rosales and Jobe). In his somewhat didactic fashion, he tried to curb his friend's occasional drinking binges (Jacob: 111).

Location: 18th and E streets N.W., in Rawlins Park.

Major General John A. Rawlins, sculpted in bronze by Joseph A. Bailly. *Photos by Maureen R. Quinn.*

José Artigas

At one time, the Spanish empire dominated much of North and most of Central and South America. But like the other imperialist European powers, Spain gradually lost her influence in the western hemisphere to the almost inevitable process of revolution which, following the initial spark of insurrection, spreads like wildfire through a country's overseas colonies. José Artigas (1764-1850) led the fight for the independence of one of those countries, Uruguay. A charismatic leader, he culled a potent military force from the legions of Uruguay's peasants and farmers. At the peak of Uruguay's struggle for self-rule, Artigas looked up to the United States as a paragon of freedom. He supposedly carried a copy of the U.S. Constitution with him everywhere he went (Goode: 444), and he has been referred to as the George Washington of Uruguay.

The memorial to the father of Uruguayan independence was erected in 1950, the centennial of Artigas's death. The nine-foot bronze statue was sculpted by Juan M. Blanes, and the $29,000 cost was funded by Uruguayans, among them school children. Artigas is depicted in a broad stance, holding his hat in his right hand, as if he is giving a speech. His left hand rests on the pommel of his sheathed sword. The inscription on the pedestal reads "From the people of Uruguay to the people of the United States. Liberty of America is my dream and its attainment my only hope." Above the inscription is the general's name.

Secretary of State Dean Acheson formally accepted the statue, a gift from the people of Uruguay to the people of the United States, on behalf of President Harry S. Truman. Representing Uruguay was ambassador Alberto Dominguez-Campora. Following the June 19 dedication, the Uruguayan Embassy held a reception for guests at the Carlton Hotel.

Location: Constitution Avenue and 18th Street, N.W.

Korean War Veterans Memorial

In a triangular field interspersed with short, broad rows of black granite, nineteen U. S. soldiers warily advance toward an American flag. Wearing helmets and ponchos, rifles slung over their shoulders, several are glancing furtively behind them, as if expecting an enemy ambush. These stainless steel statues, by Frank Gaylord, represent fifteen Army soldiers, two Marines, one Navy medic, and one Air Force observer (NPS). Original plans called for thirty-eight statues – a reference to the 38th parallel, which separates North and South Korea – but because this was not feasible, a polished, black granite wall was added instead to reflect the images of the nineteen soldiers. The 164-foot long wall stands to the right of the platoon, and the images of 2,400 actual service men and women are sandblasted into the surface, giving the impression that they are staring back at visitors to the memorial. Inscribed at the base of the wall is "FREEDOM IS NOT FREE."

In a triangular field interspersed with short, broad rows of black granite, nineteen U. S. soldiers warily advance towards an American flag. Sculpted by Frank Gaylord, these stainless steel figures are part of the Korean War Memorial, dedicated in 1995. *Photos by Robert M. Heller and Maureen R. Quinn.*

Dedicated in 1995 to recall the veterans of "the forgotten war," the memorial occupies 2.2 acres of land in West Potomac Park. At the point of the triangular field is the thirty-foot diameter Pool of Remembrance. To the north of the stainless steel platoon, opposite the black granite wall, a walkway is inscribed with the names of the twenty-one countries who participated in the Korean War, along with casualty figures for each. The conflict was officially a United Nations' effort.

Four architects from State College, Pennsylvania, won the 1989 design competition for the Korean Veterans Memorial.

Location: Independence Avenue and 23rd Street, Potomac Park.

In 1966, the Institute of Hispanic Culture in Madrid gave the statue to the Organization of American States (OAS). Formally making the presentation on April 14 was Spanish Foreign Minister Fernando Maria Castiella. Representing the OAS was Assistant Secretary William Saunders.

Queen Isabella I. *Photos by Maureen R. Quinn.*

Queen Isabella I

Sculpted by Jose Luis Sanchez, this statue of Queen Isabella (1451-1504) almost looks like a primitive idol carved by some ancient culture. The queen's body is little more than a cylinder with a crowned head protruding. The statue's hands jut out from the center of the figure, seemingly unattached to any pair of arms. Isabella holds in front of her a pomegranate, from which a dove is hatching. The Spanish inscription in bronze letters on the cube-shaped pedestal translates:

Isabella I, the Catholic queen of Castille, of Aragon, of the islands and firm ground of the Atlantic Ocean.

Isabella was born in 1451 to King John II of Castile and Isabella of Portugal. Upon John II's death in 1454, Isabella's brother, Henry IV, ascended to the Castilian throne. Eight years later, bickering broke out over Henry's desire to name his daughter, Juana, heir to the throne of Castile, and rumors circulated that she was not Henry's daughter, but the illegitimate child of the duke of Albuquerque. Eventually, however, Henry agreed to name his sister as heir. But, when she married Ferdinand of Portugal, Henry reneged, again insisting that his daughter, Juana, be his successor. This led to a war with Portugal. At its conclusion, Isabella became queen of Castile. When Ferdinand became King of Aragon, the royal couple at last succeeded in uniting the country (Lewis).

Ferdindand and Isabella's greatest legacy is their sponsorship of the 1492 expedition of Italian sailor Christopher Columbus, a voyage that was to bring great wealth and prestige to Spain. Isabella was sympathetic toward the Native Americans, and did her utmost to insure that they were treated well, though this was understandably difficult from a distance of 5,000 miles. Her apparent benevolence toward the Indians, however, stands in stark contrast to the treatment given to "heretics" during the Spanish Inquisition, which was instituted during her reign.

Location: Constitution Avenue and 17th Street, N.W., in front of the Pan American Union Building.

Red Cross Monument (Red Cross Spirit)

June 25, 1959 marked nine years to the day that North Korean troops crossed the 38th parallel, invading their southern neighbors and precipitating a "police action" that would drag on for three years and claim thousands of lives. On that summer day nine years later, the Korean War was still fresh in the minds of those who attended a dedication ceremony for a monument to Red Cross workers killed in the line of duty. That may have been the reason for choosing that specific date, which coincidentally marked the eighty-third anniversary of General George Custer's last stand at the Battle of Little Bighorn.

Presiding was General Mark W. Clark, president of The Citadel military college in Charleston, South Carolina, and commander of the United States Fifth Army in Italy during the Second World War. Clark reminded those in attendance that although the Red Cross was best known for courageous humanitarian efforts during times of conflict, the organization was always ready to assist the needy, in peace as well as war. Natural disasters, Clark said, were also cause for Red Cross workers to spring into action.

Accepting the memorial on behalf of the American Red Cross was the organization's national chairman, E. Roland Harriman. The dedication ceremony was preceded by a performance from the U.S. Marine Corps Band. Following the ceremony, the memorial was unveiled by a retired Red Cross worker, and the assistant director of the organization's nursing services in Washington, D.C.

Felix de Weldon's bronze sculpture group depicts two men carrying an injured soldier, while a woman in the middle tends to his wounds. The men who are lifting the soldier are clearly struggling with their burden, and the soldier's face conveys his agony. Each of the figures is approximately seven feet tall. Inscribed on the five-foot marble base is:

> IN HONOR AND MEMORY OF THE MEN AND WOMEN OF THE AMERICAN RED CROSS WHO HAVE GIVEN THEIR LIVES IN THE SERVICE OF MANKIND IN PEACE AND WAR.

Five years earlier, De Weldon's immense Iwo Jima memorial had been unveiled at Arlington National Cemetery. At the time of De Weldon's death in 2003, he had over 1,000 monuments to his credit. His other works in the District include the Simon Bolivar statue at E and 18th streets and the Veterans of Foreign Wars memorial at the intersection of 2nd Street and Constitution and Maryland avenues.

The Red Cross Spirit was erected by the American Red Cross Overseas Association (ARCOA), to commemorate the nearly 300 Red Cross personnel who were killed in World Wars I, II, and the Korean War. No figures are available for how many died between the organization's founding in 1881 and 1914.

Location: Red Cross Square, former American Red Cross headquarters, E and 17th streets, N.W.

Felix de Weldon's 1959 tribute to Red Cross workers who have died in the line of duty. *Photo courtesy of American Red Cross. All rights reserved in all countries.*

Signers of the Declaration of Independence Monument

The delegates who assembled at the third Continental Congress in Philadelphia during the summer of 1776 had a daunting decision before them: whether or not to approve a declaration officially severing ties with the mother country. There had been intermittent clashes with British forces during the past year, but efforts at resolving the crisis peacefully had not as of yet been abandoned. By signing a document declaring that the thirteen colonies – Connecticut, Delaware, Georgia, Maryland, Massachusetts, New Hampshire, New Jersey, New York, North Carolina, Pennsylvania, Rhode Island, South Carolina, and Virginia – now constituted a separate country, the delegates knew that there was no turning back.

Thomas Jefferson drew up the document, relying on suggestions and input from Benjamin Franklin. Jefferson gave a litany of justifications for the schism with Great Britain, accusing George III of a number of wrongs, including forcing colonists to house British troops, allowing crimes committed against Americans by British soldiers to go unpunished, and trying Americans in England for infractions allegedly committed on American soil. Interesting to note is that in the second paragraph of the final draft, Jefferson asserts that "all men are created equal," yet several paragraphs later, when accusing the king of inciting Indians to attack the colonists, refers to Native Americans as "merciless Indian savages."

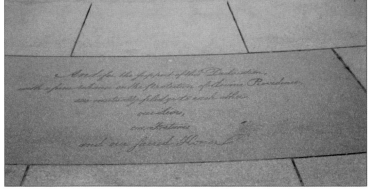

This monument to the Signers of the Declaration of Independence was installed for the nation's bicentennial in 1976. *Photos by Janet L. Greentree.*

From old to modern times, lawyers have tended to dominate politics, and of the fifty-six signers of the Declaration of Independence, nearly half of them were lawyers or judges. Other signers included a number of merchants, farmers, and four physicians. All were aware of the great risk that they were taking by committing what was tantamount to treason as far as the Crown was concerned. Several of the their homes and properties were looted during the revolution, and a number of the signers' died paupers.

In 1976, a monument most appropriate for the nation's bicentennial was installed at Constitution Avenue and 19th Street, in Constitution Gardens. This memorial consists of a granite plaza inscribed with reproduced signatures of the fifty-six signers of the Declaration of Independence.

Location: Constitution Avenue and 19th Street, in Constitution Gardens.

Simon Bolivar

Simon Bolivar (1783-1830) spent about fifteen years fighting for independence from Spain for several South American countries, one of which is named for him. He was the first president of Greater Colombia, which consisted of the present-day countries of Venezuela, Peru, Ecuador, and Bolivia. Bolivar's popularity declined, however, and this eventually led to Venezuela and Ecuador's seceding from the newly-formed country.

Created by Felix de Weldon, the bronze equestrian statue shows Bolivar charging into battle, his heels straining at the stirrups, his sword raised high above his head. Inscribed on the front of the black marble pedestal is "SIMON BOLIVAR/ THE LIBERATOR," and beneath that, dates and places of his birth and death. The memorial was dedicated in 1958.

Location: E and 18th streets.

Simon Bolivar. *Photos by Maureen R. Quinn.*

Vietnam Veterans Memorial

In the wake of the most divisive war that the United States had ever fought, a group of veterans headed by Jan Scruggs formed an organization to establish a memorial honoring the millions of Americans who had served, and the tens of thousands who had died during the twelve-year conflict. Four years had passed since the last American troops had pulled out of Vietnam, and although the war was officially over, the healing process had barely begun. In 1980, three acres were set aside in Constitution Gardens for the erection of a memorial. One of the criterion for a 1981 design competition was that the memorial be free of any political bias regarding American involvement in the war. The winning design was submitted by twenty-one-year-old Yale University architecture student Maya Ying Lin.

Lin's design was praised for both its stark simplicity and natural beauty. Two black granite walls built into an embankment come together to form a "V," the ends of which point toward the Washington Monument and Lincoln Memorial respectively. Each wall is 246 feet, eight inches long, and 10 feet, one-and-a-half inches at their apex. Beginning where the east and west walls meet are inscribed the names of the more than 58,000 Americans killed or missing in action. The names are in chronological and alphabetical order, starting on the east wall with 1959 and ending on the west wall with 1975. Those confirmed killed are denoted with a diamond, while those whose whereabouts remain unknown are marked with a cross. Each wall is divided into seventy panels. A granite walkway runs along the wall. Lin called the memorial "a rift in the earth – a long, polished, black stone wall, emerging from and receding into the earth" (Kohler: 126). Construction began in March of 1982, and the Wall was dedicated on Memorial Day of the same year. The project was funded entirely by donations.

Not everyone was enamored with Lin's concept, however. One Vietnam veteran called the wall "a black gash of shame." Other detractors attacked the memorial as too simplistic, claiming that it lacked an element of humanity. In part as a response to the latter criticism, "The Three Servicemen" sculpture was added in 1984. The work of the late Frederick Hart, the sculpture is composed of three bronze statues of American soldiers – one white, one black, and one Hispanic. Hart's design for the original memorial had won third place in the 1981 competition. The faces of the soldiers reflect both the strained stoicism and thinly-veiled fear of young men thrown into the brutality of war. As was the case with the Wall, there was controversy over the addition of the Three Servicemen, with critics calling the sculp-

ture extraneous, and detracting from the power of Lin's design. Proponents won out, however, and the new sculpture, as well as a flagpole, were dedicated that November, also on Memorial Day. An American flag flies twenty-four hours a day at the Vietnam Veterans Memorial.

"The Wall" contains the names of 58,000 Americans killed or missing in action during the Vietnam War. *Photo by Robert M. Heller.*

Every year, hundreds of offerings are left at the Wall – flowers, dog tags, medals, teddy bears, toys, and photographs. Park rangers regularly collect the items, which are then transferred to the Museum Resource Center in Landover, Maryland.

Location: Constitution Gardens, in West Potomac Park, south of Constitution Avenue and east of Henry Bacon Drive Northwest.

On a clear spring day, visitors gather to pay their respects at the Vietnam Memorial.
Photo by Robert M. Heller.

Frederick Hart's Three Servicemen sculpture, added in 1984. *Photo by Maureen R. Quinn.*

Vietnam Women's Memorial

For Diane Carlson Evans, and the 12,000 other women who had served in Vietnam, eight names lost in a black granite sea of 58,000 similar inscriptions hardly seemed a fitting tribute. In 1984, the former Army nurse established the Vietnam Women's Memorial Project to construct a tribute bestowing recognition commensurate with that of their brother soldiers, who had been memorialized by Maya Ying Lin's impressive V-shaped wall and Frederick Hart's starkly realistic Three Servicemen sculpture. The organization later became the Vietnam Women's Memorial Foundation.

Near a sixty-foot flagpole on the grounds of the Vietnam Veterans Memorial is a bronze sculpture depicting three military women. One of the women, seated on a pile of sandbags, is caring for a wounded soldier, while a second woman looks skyward. The third woman is kneeling, perhaps in prayer, or to take a moment to gather her thoughts and make sense of the horror and futility which surround her. Near the statue are eight yellowwood trees, symbolizing the eight American women who died during the Vietnam War. Their names were Mary Therese Klinker, Eleanor Grace Alexander, Hedwig Diane Orlowski, Carol Ann Elizabeth Drazba, Elizabeth Ann Jones, Pamela Dorothy Donovan, Annie Ruth Graham, and Sharon Ann Lane. All of these women were nurses, seven from the Army and one, Mary Therese Klinker, from the Air Force. In addition to the eight nurses, over fifty civilian women lost their lives in Vietnam. Sculptor Glenna Goodacre's design was chosen from among 317 entries in a competition.

The dedication of the Vietnam Women's Memorial on Veterans Day in 1993 marked the end of a long and contentious struggle. Many people questioned the need for a separate memorial for women. Among them was Maya Ying Lin, who implied that its addition would spark efforts by special interest and minority groups to each campaign for their own separate memorial. Frederick Hart was also opposed to the idea. In 1987, women who served in Vietnam argued their case before the Commission of Fine Arts. The following year, President Ronald W. Reagan signed a bill authorizing a memorial to the American women who had served during the Vietnam War.

Location: Constitution Gardens, in West Potomac Park, south of Constitution Avenue and east of Henry Bacon Drive Northwest, on the grounds of the Vietnam Veterans Memorial.

The Vietnam Women's Memorial was installed in 1993, following extensive lobbying by women veterans. On the grounds are eight yellowwood trees, representing the eight nurses who lost their lives during the Vietnam War. Copyright 1993, Vietnam Women's Memorial Foundation. Sculptor Glenna Goodacre. *Photo courtesy of Cindy Gurney.*

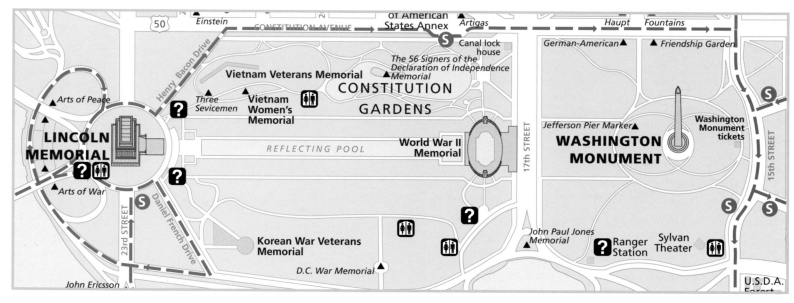

Map locating most of the statues and monuments discussed in this section of the guide.
Map courtesy of the National Park Service, U.S. Department of the Interior.

3c From the Washington Monument to the Lincoln Memorial

John Paul Jones

The late, great Commodore John Paul Jones is one of a host of American heroes of the Revolutionary War who was not born in America. He was born John Paul on July 6, 1747, and later added the surname "Jones." The stalwart Scotsman entered the annals of history with his defiant response when during a September 23, 1779, naval battle, the commander of the British ship *Serapis* asked him to surrender the *Bonhomme Richard*. "Surrender? I have not yet begun to fight!" Jones retorted. Richard Pearson, the captain of the *Serapis*, eventually surrendered to Jones. At the time, Jones was a captain in the Continental Navy. After the war, Jones enlisted as a rear admiral in the Russian navy. He died in 1792, at the age of forty-five. In 1905, the legendary maritime hero was exhumed from his pauper's grave in France and re-interred in the grounds of the United States Naval Academy in Annapolis, Maryland.

Naval hero John Paul Jones, sculpted by Charles Henry Niehaus. *Photo by Maureen R. Quinn.*

History often becomes clouded with the passing of many years, and some question arose whether Jones really uttered his famous quote verbatim. This was due to the fact that one of his officers was recounting the incident to a biographer of Jones nearly half a century after the alleged incident. Regardless of what his exact words were, the intent of those words and the result of the battle remain unchanged (Bowen-Haskell et al.: 47).

The Jones statue stands in front of a shallow rectangular alcove in a large marble shaft. He is depicted in his naval uniform and tri-cornered hat. On the rear of the marble shaft is a bas-relief of Jones raising a flag on his ship, while his crew looks on in admiration. Above this scene is his famous reply to the enemy, and beneath, the inscription: "IN LIFE HE HONORED/ THE FLAG. IN DEATH THE/FLAG SHALL HONOR HIM."

Congress appropriated $50,000 to for the bronze memorial, which was designed by Thomas Hastings and sculpted by Charles Henry Niehaus. Niehaus, a talented, if somewhat peevish artist, had several prominent works to recommend him, among them the Samuel Hahnemann memorial in Scott Circle, which he had completed twelve years earlier. His first commission had been for a statue of James Garfield for the city of Cincinnati.

Location: 17th Street and Independence Avenue, in West Potomac Park.

Lincoln Memorial

As was the case with the Washington Monument, the Lincoln Memorial was in the planning stages long before its actual construction, which began in 1914. Designed by architect Henry Bacon, the memorial was modeled after the Parthenon in Athens, but also calls to mind one of the Seven Wonders of the Ancient World – the statue of Zeus in the temple at Olympia, in western Greece.

Thirty-six forty-four-foot high Doric columns, representing the number of states in the Union when Lincoln was president, adorn this shrine to the father of emancipation. The frieze on the building is inscribed with the names of the nation's forty-eight states when the memorial was dedicated. In 1982, a plaque listing Alaska and Hawaii was added to the lower terrace.

Resting atop a ten-foot pedestal, the seated statue of Lincoln is nineteen feet tall, and was assembled from twenty-eight separate pieces of white Georgia marble. One story purports that because sculptor Daniel Chester French had a deaf child, he designed the president's hands to form the letters "A" and "L" in sign language (WCTC). Others maintain that French did this to honor Thomas Hopkins Gallaudet, for whom the District's Gallaudet University for the deaf is named (RWM).

On the south wall, to the right of where Lincoln is seated, is inscribed the Gettysburg Address, and on the north wall, Lincoln's second inaugural speech. Above the Gettysburg Address is Jules Guerin's mural of an angel liberating a slave; above Lincoln's second inaugural speech, a mural depicting the unification of the country. Inscribed on the wall behind Lincoln is:

IN THIS TEMPLE/AS IN THE HEARTS OF THE PEOPLE/FOR WHOM HE SAVED THE UNION/THE MEMORY OF ABRAHAM LINCOLN/IS ENSHRINED FOREVER.

It was on the granite steps of the Lincoln Memorial that Martin Luther King, Jr. gave his famous "I have a dream" speech in 1963, and where, twenty-four years earlier, singer Marian Anderson gave a free concert for a crowd of 75,000. However, when the Lincoln Memorial was dedicated on Memorial Day in 1922, blacks who attended were forced to sit in a segregated section.

The Lincoln Memorial has been the site of rallies, protests, demonstrations, and celebrations for over eighty years. *Photos by Maureen R. Quinn.*

The Lincoln Memorial sits on 6.3 acres at the west end of the Reflecting Pool, opposite the Washington Monument on the east end. Several possible sites, among them Arlington National Cemetery, were discussed before the Commission of Fine Arts settled on the eventual location. A bridge leads from the Lincoln Memorial, across the Potomac River, to Arlington National Cemetery.

Location: 23rd Street and Daniel Chester French Drive S.W., West Potomac Park, west end of the Reflecting Pool.

Daniel Chester French's massive marble sculpture of Abraham Lincoln was assembled from twenty-eight separate pieces. *Photo by Maureen R. Quinn.*

Washington Monument

Rising 555 feet, this marble obelisk is the tallest structure in Washington, D.C, and when completed, was the tallest struc-

ture in the world. During the last years of George Washington's life, there was support for the erection of a monument in his honor. As early as 1783, the Continental Congress approved an equestrian statue of the first president for the official monument, though this idea was obviously not used. Ambitious architect Robert Mills began work on the design in 1836, but lack of funding and changes in the plan delayed construction for twelve years. Then in 1852, the project was suspended, again due to lack of funds. The unfinished monument was then 170 feet tall. Work resumed in 1876, but did not progress fast enough for some Washingtonians. In a December 19, 1877 letter to the editor of *The Washington Post*, one reader complained:

> Near the filthy marsh in the rear of the White House ... stands an unsightly stone structure called by jobbers a "Monument to the Immortal Washington." For thirty years it has stood there, a disgrace to the name of the father of his country, and a course to the Nation.

Mills had died in 1855, and the resumption of work on the monument was supervised by the Army Corps of Engineers. Because the original vein of marble from the quarry was depleted, a slightly different colored marbled was used to complete the remainder of the monument, but only a keen eye will spot this. The cap on the one-and-a-half-ton capstone is made of aluminum.

The dedication came on George Washington's birthday in 1885, and the Washington Monument opened to the public in 1888. The first visitors had to climb 897 steps to get to the lookout station at the top. Along the way, they could observe the 192 memorial stones set into the interior walls, listing the names of individuals, businesses, and even foreign countries who helped finance the construction. Later, a very sluggish elevator was added, and was eventually replaced by a much faster one. Due to security concerns and public health considerations, climbing the stairs is no longer permitted. Flashing red lights on the capstone were installed to alert passing aircraft. In 1959, flags for all fifty states were added around the base of the monument.

Location: West Mall and 15th Street, Potomac Park.

At 555 feet, the Washington Monument is the tallest structure in the capital. *Photo by Maureen R. Quinn.*

The Reflecting Pool shimmers in the twilight.
Photos by Maureen R. Quinn.

World War I Memorial

The passage of time and erection of the World War II Memorial in April of 2005 has overshadowed this monument commemorating the men of the District of Columbia killed in the First World War. The structure is a marble dome supported by fluted columns. The frieze bears the insignia of the various armed forces.

The United States entered World War I in July of 1917. The country had resisted pressure to join the fighting, but after the interception of the Zimmermann Telegram by British intelligence (see Friedrich von Steuben, p. 73), decided that there was no alternative. By the time of the armistice sixteen months later, American losses totaled over 50,000.

Location: Independence Avenue and Ohio Drive, in Potomac Park.

The passage of time and erection of the massive World War II Memorial in April of 2005 has overshadowed this monument commemorating the men of the District of Columbia killed in the First World War. *Photos by Maureen R. Quinn.*

World War II Memorial

More so than any other conflict in history, the Second World War has become thoroughly ingrained in the human psyche. The rumbling of German discord that began in the wake of their defeat in 1918, coupled with Japanese invasions of the Chinese mainland, eventually exploded into worldwide pandemonium. For six long years, war rolled like a juggernaut across Europe, Asia, and Africa. No country, even those that vowed complete neutrality, would remain unaffected.

Memorials and tributes to World War II dead have sprung up all over the country. These monuments often commemorate residents of a particular town, county or organization. The quintessential World War II memorial was finally dedicated on Veterans Day in 2004, eleven years after President William J. Clinton signed a law authorizing its construction. Vast in scope and scale, the memorial honors the sixteen million Americans who served in the conflict, and the 400,000 who lost their lives. The construction took three years, and cost nearly $200 million, most of which came from donations. Senator Bob Dole, who was seriously wounded during the war, chaired the fundraising committee. As of the writing of this book in April 2005, the tribute to World War II veterans was Washington, D.C.'s newest memorial.

Many people find the $200 million World War II Memorial to be excessive and grandiose. *Photo by Maureen R. Quinn.*

The World War II Memorial is designed around a large oval, with a pool in the center, and a fountain at either end of the pool. Around the perimeter of the "Rainbow Pool" are tiny jets of water. On one of the surrounding granite walls is a quote from President Dwight D. Eisenhower encouraging the troops prior to the June 6, 1944 D-Day invasion. The Freedom Wall, located on the eastern edge of the memorial, features 4,000 gold stars, set in a field of blue, each star representing 100 Americans killed in action. At the base of the Freedom Wall is a raised curb with the inscription "HERE WE MARK THE PRICE OF FREEDOM." Two granite pavilions – designated as "Atlantic" and "Pacific" – stand at the south and north ends of the memorial, respectively. The interior of each pavilion features four bronze eagles holding in their beaks a ribbon, which is wrapped around a memorial wreath. On each side of the Atlantic and Pacific pavilions are 14 pillars – for a total of fifty-six – with the names of America's states and territories during the Second World War. Some 17,000 blocks of granite were used in assembling the memorial (wwiimemorial.com). The foundation is concrete.

Construction was overseen by the American Battle Monuments Commission. After completion, the memorial was officially turned over to the jurisdiction of the National Park Service.

Location: 17th Street, between Independence and Constitution avenues, west of the Washington Monument, and east of the Lincoln Memorial.

Behind the Rainbow Pool, which is the center of the memorial, is the Freedom Wall, which bears 4,000 gold stars. Each star represents 100 American lives lost during World War II. *Photos by Maureen R. Quinn.*

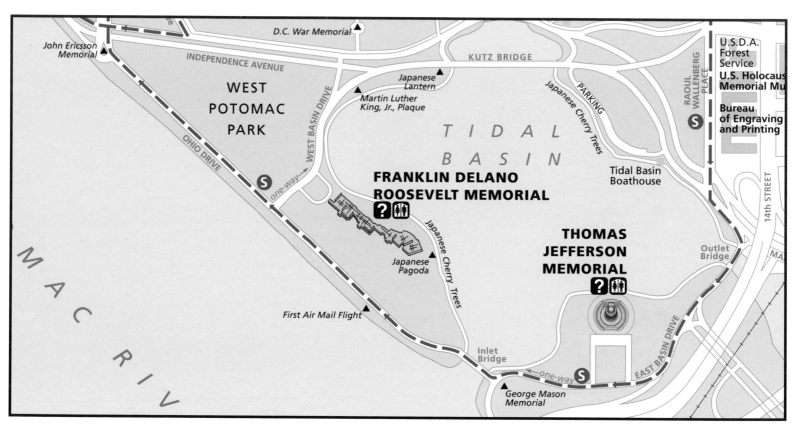

Map locating most of the statues and monuments discussed in this section of the guide.
Map courtesy of the National Park Service, U.S. Department of the Interior.

③d The Tidal Basin

Cuban American Friendship Urn/ U.S.S. *Maine* Memorial

Tangible legacies often outlast intangible ones. People are born and die, political climates change, old alliances are broken and new ones forged. "... [Y]et stones have stood for a thousand years," wrote poet Robinson Jeffers. Considering the poor relationship between the United States and Cuba today, "Cuban American Friendship Urn" seems an awkward name for this memorial, which was presented to the United States by the Cuban government in 1928. Also known as the U.S.S. *Maine* Memorial, it was originally created to commemorate the loss of American sailors on that ship, which sunk off the coast of the tiny island nation thirty years earlier. While President Calvin Coolidge was on an official visit to Havana, Cuban president Gerardo Machado y Morales discussed giving the urn to the United States, as Coolidge later said "as a testimony of friendship and appreciation of the Cuban government" (*Washington Post*). The seven-foot high, six-ton marble urn was carved from a larger memorial in Havana. Later, it was moved to the grounds of the Cuban Embassy, and finally, to the present location in Potomac Park, at 14th Street and Ohio Drive. The pedestal was created separately. Around the sides of the urn are various memorial plaques in Spanish. In 1913, a memorial to the U.S.S. *Maine* was erected in New York City's Columbus Circle. There are also memorials in Arlington National Cemetery and at the United States Naval Academy in Annapolis, Maryland.

Originally intended to commemorate the 258 U.S. sailors killed in the loss of the U.S.S. *Maine*, the Cuban-American Friendship Urn was given to the United States by Cuba in 1928 "as a testimony of friendship and appreciation of the Cuban government." *Photos by Maureen R. Quinn.*

The U.S.S. *Maine* blew up on February 15, 1898 in Havana Harbor, killing 258 sailors. On the following morning, the tangled wreckage was still visible in the shallow waters where the *Maine* sank. The ship at that time was eight years old. The explosion was most likely an accident, and eighty years later, Admiral Hyman Rickover put forth the theory that a fire in a coal bunker had ignited a cache of munitions. But in 1898, headlines in American newspapers screamed that Spanish saboteurs were to blame, accusations backed by then Assistant Secretary of the Navy, Theodore Roosevelt. Spanish denials were subsequently ignored. "Remember the *Maine*; to hell with Spain!" became the rallying cry of an enraged American public. The ensuing conflict lasted a short six months, and ended with Spain's loss of Cuba and the Philippines.

Location: 14th Street and Ohio Drive, in Potomac Park.

Franklin Delano Roosevelt Memorial

Hailed by some as the savior of democracy and free enterprise, condemned by others as a socialist, Franklin Delano Roosevelt has secured a prominent place in the annals of American history. The former senator and governor of New York was elected the country's thirty-second president during the worst economic crisis that the nation had ever faced. To spur recovery from the Great Depression, he instituted sweeping public works programs that employed millions of displaced workers. After leading his country through the darkest days of World War II, he died of a cerebral hemorrhage in April of 1945, four months shy of an Allied victory.

Twenty-five years after his passing, the decision came to erect a memorial to the late FDR. In 1960, the Roosevelt Memorial Commission held a design contest. The winning entry, submitted by a New York City architectural firm, consisted of a series of raised concrete slabs of varying heights and positions, inscribed with some of Roosevelt's more famous quotes. But after the Roosevelt family expressed their disapproval of the design, the project lapsed into limbo for over ten years. The job was eventually entrusted to California architect Lawrence Halprin, although sixteen years passed between the submission of Halprin's original plans and the start of construction.

The memorial was built between 1991 and 1997. During that time, 6,000 tons of granite were quarried from South Dakota for the construction. The memorial contains four rooms, symbolic of Roosevelt's record four terms in office, from 1933 to 1945. Throughout the four rooms in the memorial, Halprin uses water for added symbolic effect, and 100,000 gallons continuously flow through the structure (NPS). The granite hallways connecting the rooms are inscribed with quotations of the late president.

The FDR Memorial features a statue of former First Lady, Eleanor Roosevelt. *Photo by Maureen R. Quinn.*

The Prologue Room of the FDR Memorial. *Photo by Maureen R. Quinn.*

The FDR memorial recalls the hard times of the Great Depression. *Photos by Maureen R. Quinn.*

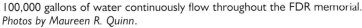

100,000 gallons of water continuously flow throughout the FDR memorial. *Photos by Maureen R. Quinn.*

Changing social attitudes played a part in the design, as well. In 2001, designers bowed to pressure from groups representing the disabled and at the entrance to the monument added a statue of FDR in his wheelchair. While in his late thirties, Roosevelt had been crippled by a bout of polio. In addition, FDR was seldom without his cigarette in its long, slender holder, but this is noticeably absent from his statue. The statue of Eleanor Roosevelt in the fourth room depicts the First Lady without her fur wrap (Rambow: 17).

The memorial also has a statue of Roosevelt's Scottish terrier, Fala. Visitors sometimes rub Fala's nose for good luck. The ten bronze statues throughout the memorial were sculpted by Neil Estern.

Although FDR is credited with creating Social Security, a similar system was put in place in the nineteenth century by Prussian chancellor Otto von Bismark.

Location: Independence Avenue and Ohio Drive, in Potomac Park.

The Braille Wall at the FDR memorial.
Photos by Maureen R. Quinn.

George Mason National Memorial

George Mason bore no animosity toward his fellow Virginians George Washington and Thomas Jefferson. Likely he still considered them friends, but a rift unquestionably came between them over Mason's refusal to sign the Constitution. A staunch anti-federalist, Mason served as a delegate to the Constitutional Convention in 1787, and forcefully argued that the Constitution in its present form gave too much authority to the central government. But Washington, Jefferson, and others desperately wanted their new country to be composed of "united" states. During and even after the Revolutionary War, the colonies were more like thirteen separate countries, and the fact that they were able to work together to defeat a common enemy was quite a task (PBS). To appease the stubborn, stodgy Mason, the Bill of Right was added to the Constitution in 1791, but even this did not completely smooth matters over.

An existing park, circa the 1920s, formed the backdrop for the George Mason National Memorial, which was dedicated on April 9, 2002. Some modifications were made to the park's fountain, and a significant number of flowers and shrubs were planted. A long oval of grass, bounded by concrete walkways, stretches before the bronze statue of George Mason underneath a long colonnade formed by sixteen pillars supporting a metal trellis. In the exact center of the colonnade, the pensive figure of Mason sits, legs crossed, on a large stone bench. To his right are his cane and hat, and he is holding a book. Inscribed on the end of a concrete curb which surrounds roughly half of the grassy oval are the words: "George Mason. 1725-1792. Author of America's first bill of rights." On either side of Mason are four-foot by twelve-foot stone walls with eight of his more famous quotes, and one quote from Thomas Jefferson, as well. Sculptor Wendy M. Ross of Bethesda, Maryland, created the bronze Mason, and architect Faye B. Harwell of Alexandria, Virginia, designed the landscaping. The $2.1 million cost was funded by donations to the Board of Regents of Gunston Hall Plantation, Mason's Virginia estate.

A seated, bronze George Mason seems to be enjoying his park surroundings. *Photo by Maureen R. Quinn.*

George Mason, father of the Bill of Rights, rendered in bronze in 2002 by Bethesda, Maryland, sculptor Wendy M. Ross. *Photos by Maureen R. Quinn.*

Mason claimed to be against slavery, and wanted specific prohibitions added to the Constitution. One of the quotes inscribed on the walls deals with his ostensible opposition to the practice. Incredibly, however, Mason himself owned slaves, a hypocrisy not lost on modern observers (Forgey, Willogoren).

Location: 14th Street Bridge and Ohio Drive, S.W.

Jefferson Memorial

Although he predeceased the venerable Abraham Lincoln by almost forty years, Thomas Jefferson was to wait another twenty-one years before he, too, was enshrined in a Classical temple. Designed by John Russell Pope, whose credits include the Second Division Monument at Constitution Avenue and 17th Street and the National Gallery of Art, the white marble structure that houses the nineteen-foot bronze statue of Jefferson was modeled after the Pantheon in Greece. Jefferson was something of an architect himself, and very much a fan of Classical architecture, as is evidenced by the design of his Monticello. No doubt he would have approved.

Sculpted by Rudolph Evans, Jefferson stands on a six-foot marble platform, under a domed roof supported by twenty-six Ionic columns. In his left hand, he is holding the Declaration of Independence as he addresses the Continental Congress. The long fur coat that he is sporting is a gift from his friend, General Thaddeus Kosciuszko.

Overcoming the internecine bickering that frequently occurs with large, collaborative projects was one of many hurdles that planners faced. The Commission of Fine Arts was not keen on the Pantheon-style design, and there were the usual debates over location. Some district residents objected to building the memorial on the edge of the tidal basin, then called Twining Lake. They did not want any of the beautiful cherry blossom trees, which had been a gift from Japan in 1912, to be cut down. Eventually, very few of the trees had to be removed to accommodate the memorial. In 1937, the death of Pope caused another setback, but architects Otto R. Eggers and Daniel P. Higgins were able to take over where Pope had left off. Still, plans for completing the memorial by April 13, 1943 – Jefferson's 200th birthday – proved to be too ambitious. The dedication proceeded as planned, with President Franklin Delano Roosevelt's presiding, but because the bronze that was used to create the statue of Jefferson could not be spared during the Second World War, the five-ton sculpture was not completed until four years later.

A fellow Virginian and contemporary of George Washington, Jefferson was the third president of the United States, from 1801 to 1809. Prior to that, he had served as John Adams's vice president after unsuccessfully running against him in 1796. His greatest achievement as president was perhaps his 1803 Louisiana Purchase from France, which doubled the territory of the United States. Despite his status as a Founding Father, the wealthy slave owner has been assailed with posthumous allegations of hypocrisy and racism.

An avid reader and man of letters, Jefferson accumulated a personal library containing thousands of books on diverse subjects. After British troops burned the White House in 1814 and destroyed the collection of the Library of Congress, Jefferson sold the government his personal library at cost. Perhaps appropriately, Jefferson died at his Monticello estate on July 4, 1826 – his country's fiftieth birthday. Within hours, second President John Adams had also expired. The two men shared a mutual contempt, and even when Jefferson was Adams's vice president, they managed to associate as little as possible. On his deathbed, Adams was unaware that Jefferson had died earlier that day, and supposedly voiced his dismay that he himself was dying, while his nemesis was still alive (Independence Hall Association).

Location: Basin and Ohio drives, at the edge of the Tidal Basin, in Potomac Park.

The white marble structure that houses the nineteen-foot bronze statue of Jefferson was modeled after the Pantheon in Greece. *Photos by Maureen R. Quinn.*

Rudolph Evans's massive sculpture of Thomas Jefferson was not completed until four years after the April 13, 1943 dedication of the memorial. This was because of a shortage of bronze due to World War II. *Photos by Maureen R. Quinn.*

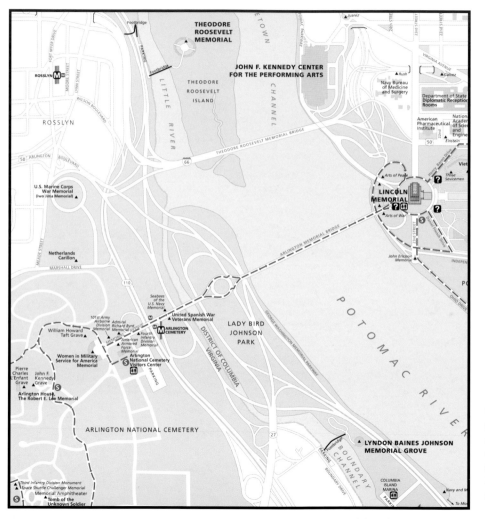

Map locating most of the statues and monuments discussed in this section of the guide. *Map courtesy of the National Park Service, U.S. Department of the Interior.*

3e Crossing the Potomac: National Cemetery and the Environs

Iwo Jima/United States Marine Corps Memorial

Misunderstandings persist about the February 23, 1945 flag-raising on Mount Suribachi. Although Felix de Weldon's immense sculpture depicts four Marines hoisting an American flag, there were six – John Bradley, Rene Gagnon, Ira Hayes, Mike Strank, Harlon Block, and Franklin Sousey. Strank and Gagnon are barely visible in the back row of Joe Rosenthal's Pulitzer Prize-winning photograph. In addition, this dramatic event was actually the second flag-raising atop the 550-foot peak, as a smaller flag had been hoisted earlier by a different group of Marines, then taken town and replaced. Thirdly, although an American victory was close at hand, the battle was not over when the second flag was raised. In fact, Strank, Block, and Sousey would die hours later, and Bradley would be injured by a mortar explosion. Rosenthal also took another photograph, with a large group of jubilant Marines gathered around the flagpole, brandishing their rifles and waving their helmets triumphantly. The soldiers obviously posed for this picture, but the first shot was not staged.

Dedicated on Memorial Day in 1954, De Weldon's sculpture consists of four thirty-two-foot figures hoisting a sixty-foot pole, from which flies a cloth flag. Beneath the figures are the words "UNCOMMON VALOR WAS A COMMON VIRTUE." The base is granite. The surviving flag-raisers modeled for De Weldon when he was drawing up the original designs. The bronze pieces for the memorial were cast at a foundry in New York City and shipped by truck to Arlington, Virginia. Officially known as the United States Marine Corps Memorial, this remarkable tribute cost $850,000, which was raised privately.

The bloody, five-week struggle for control of an eight square-mile island 650 miles southeast of Tokyo began in January, 1945. Although outnumbered four-to-one by American forces, the 21,000 Japanese soldiers were entrenched in concrete pillboxes and subterranean bunkers, from which they could barrage the invaders with withering fire. The Japanese had been told by their commanding officers to expect to die, but that each soldier should kill at least ten Americans first. Close to 7,000 U.S. troops lost their lives in the battle for Iwo Jima, and nearly all of the Japanese defenders perished, as well. Of the surviving Marines, nearly 18,000 were wounded.

Bradley, Gagnon, and Hayes became instant heroes after the photographic proliferation of their moment of glory. People rushed to congratulate them or shake their hands, and the press hounded them for interviews. But after enduring several weeks of living hell on that tiny South Pacific outpost, they were never quite the same, haunted by what they had seen and by their friends who never came back. Hayes fared worst of all, drinking himself to death months after the memorial's dedication. John Bradley, the last surviving flag-raiser, died in 1994, at the age of seventy.

Location: Arlington National Cemetery, Arlington, Virginia.

Erected at a cost of $850,000, this memorial pays tribute to the brave flag raisers in Joe Rosenthal's famous photograph, as well as to the 7,000 Marines who perished in the battle for Iwo Jima in 1945. *Photo by Maureen R. Quinn.*

Overlooking Arlington National Cemetery, four bronze Marines strain to raise a flag under a cloudy spring sky. Officially known as the U.S. Marine Corps Memorial, this is perhaps Felix de Weldon's most famous sculpture. *Photo by Maureen R. Quinn.*

John Ericsson

James Earle Fraser's superb memorial to engineer John Ericsson may have been the impetus for Fraser's receiving some half-dozen more sculpture commissions over the next two decades. A disciple of the great Augustus Saint-Gaudens, Fraser is known for his Authority of Law and Contemplation of Justice statues, which flank the steps of the Supreme Court (see previous entries). The creation of great art often take great amounts of time, and Fraser was unable to complete the piece by the May 1926 dedication. Instead, he simply painted a plaster mold pink to look like the type of granite used for the monument, and he finished the work the following year. Fraser received $60,000 for his efforts. Among those at the dedication were President Calvin Coolidge, and members of the Swedish royal family.

Fraser incorporated a strong element of Norse mythology into his design. A six and a half-foot seated figure of Ericsson rests atop a fifteen-and-a-half-foot granite pedestal. Directly behind Ericsson, the personifications of Vision, Adventure, and Labor stand with their backs against Yggdrassil – known as the Tree of the Universe – looking out in all directions. In the forefront is Vision, depicted as a sultry young woman, naked from the waist up, a slipping blanket covering her lower torso and legs. Adventure is an armored warrior, his left flank protected by a large shield, his right hand firmly gripping a sword. Labor is a stoic, shirtless, muscular man, eager to begin whatever task awaits him. The sculpture rests on a round pedestal, which in turns sits on a fifty by fifty-foot block, on which a compass is engraved. The inscription on the monument incorrectly credits Ericsson with inventing the screw propeller, which he only perfected.

Sculpted by the great James Earle Fraser, the brooding figure of Swedish engineer John Ericsson sits beneath the sultry personification of Vision. *Photos by Maureen R. Quinn.*

Scandinavian-Americans were fiercely-proud of the contributions of their native son, as were his countrymen. Ericsson's work on the screw propeller greatly facilitated propulsion for naval vessels. In 1861, fears about the iron-clad Confederate vessel Merrimac prompted the United States Navy to seek Ericsson's help. Ericsson designed the Monitor, which clashed with its Confederate counterpart in March of 1862. The Merrimac finally withdrew, but the confrontation was not a clear victory for either side.

The moody, often irascible Ericsson (1803-1889) had been a captain in the Swedish army prior to coming to the United States in 1839. A serious blow to his reputation came in 1844, when an accident on board a ship that he designed killed several people, including two U.S. government officials. One of the ship's guns had exploded, and even though Ericsson's design was not responsible for this, his name was tarnished by association with the tragedy.

Location: Independence Avenue and Ohio Drive S.W., in West Potomac Park.

John F. Kennedy/
The Eternal Flame

Although the clouds of Camelot which once shrouded the legacy of John Fitzgerald Kennedy have long since dissipated, the thirty-fifth president endures in the hearts and minds of his countrymen as a beacon of courage and inspiration. At best, the Kennedy years were characterized by ambition, patriotism, and bold initiative, at worst, by marital infidelity, accusations of election fraud, and his father's alleged ties to organized crime. In the final days of the Kennedy administration, the specter of war loomed over Vietnam, and in less than two years, the U.S. would send the first combat troops to the distant Southeast Asian country.

A war hero credited with saving his PT boat crew in August of 1943, Kennedy went on to political success after his stint in the military, serving in both the House of Representatives and the Senate prior to his election to the presidency. He became both the youngest person and the first Catholic to win the nation's highest office. After being defeated by the upstart young Kennedy in 1960, Eisenhower's vice president Richard M. Nixon made the famous remark that would later return to haunt him: "They won't have Richard Nixon to kick around any more."

But in spite of political triumphs and tremendous wealth, power, and prestige, the Kennedy family history has been marred repeatedly by tragedy, leaving some to speculate about a "Kennedy

More than forty years after his death, four million people come to pay their respects to the thirty-fifth president every year. *Photo by Maureen R. Quinn.*

curse." Both Kennedy and his younger brother, Robert, were assassinated; his older brother, Joseph P. Kennedy, Jr., was killed in action during the Second World War; two of Kennedy's children predeceased him, and in 1999, John, Jr. died in an airplane crash.

Kennedy was fatally shot while riding in a motorcade in Dallas, Texas, on November 22, 1963, becoming the fourth president to be assassinated, and the eighth to die in office. The circumstances surrounding his shooting, and the subsequent murder of his accused assassin, have spawned myriad conspiracy theories, none of which have been conclusively proven. Kennedy was buried in Arlington National Cemetery at the insistence of his wife, Jacqueline. He and William Howard Taft, who died in 1930, are the only two presidents interred there.

An "Eternal Flame," fueled by an underground propane source, flickers continuously at the Kennedy gravesite from the center of a five-foot diameter stone, located a few feet above a memorial plaque bearing the president's name and dates of birth and death. The surrounding ground is embedded with matching rectangular blocks of white granite. The present memorial was designed by architect John Carl Warnecke, and dedicated in 1967. The new design and location of the memorial were intended to better accommodate the huge number of visitors (Arlington National Cemetery). Nearly $1.8 million was appropriated for site improvements. The Kennedy gravesite, located on a hill in Arlington National Cemetery, comprises approximately three acres. Also interred there are Jacqueline Kennedy Onassis and two of the Kennedy children. Cemetery officials estimate that annually four million people come to pay their respects.

Location: Arlington National Cemetery, Arlington, Virginia.

In 1994, former First Lady Jacqueline Kennedy Onassis was interred alongside her first husband. *Photo by Maureen R. Quinn.*

Lyndon Baines Johnson

This tribute to the thirty-sixth president of the United States is located in Lady Bird Johnson Park, on Columbia Island, in the Potomac River. A fifteen-ton, pink granite boulder forms the centerpiece of the fifteen-acre memorial grove. The towering, four-sided monolith rises like a small mountain from a cluster of white pines and azaleas. Four smaller stones surrounding the huge chunk of granite are inscribed with quotes from the late president. The boulder was quarried in Johnson's native Texas in 1974, and placed in its location with a crane in August of the following year. Original plans for a January 31, 1976 dedication proved too ambitious, and the ceremony was held on April 6 instead.

With input from the president's widow, Lady Bird Johnson, landscape architect Meade Palmer designed the memorial grove, laying out a winding, gravel path flanked by fresh plantings of rhododendrons, holly, azaleas, and several other varieties of exotic flora.

The LBJ Memorial Grove is adjacent to the busy George Washington Parkway, and speakers at the dedication had to endure frequent interruptions from the noise of passing airplanes going to and from National Airport (Smith), which is now the Ronald Reagan Airport. Addressing the crowd were President Gerald Ford, Vice President Nelson Rockefeller and his brother, Laurence, Secretary of the Interior Thomas Kleppe, and Lady Bird Johnson. The president spoke glowingly about his predecessor, the same man who had once caustically quipped that Ford was "too stupid to walk and chew gum and the same time."

Also present was Iranian ambassador Ardeshir Zahedi. Within three years, the United States would sever all diplomatic ties with Iran following the rise of the fanatical Ayatollah Ruhollah Khomeini and the storming of the United States Embassy in Tehran.

Nash Castro, an aide to the thirty-sixth president, was the national chairman of the LBJ Memorial Grove Committee. Castro contributed several hundred thousand dollars toward the upkeep of memorial grove, which is now the responsibility of the National Park Service (ibid). The memorial itself was funded by private donations.

Location: Lady Bird Johnson Park, on Columbia Island, in the Potomac River.

Navy-Marine Memorial

This memorial is dedicated to the nearly 3,000 sailors and marines killed in action during World War I. Ernesto del Piatta's aluminum sculpture shows six seagulls flying above the crest of a wave, in a line roughly forming at the top left of the wave and extending to the opposite side. The highest gull floats thirty-five feet from the ground. A seventh gull flaps in front of the breaking wave, almost blending into the rolling curves that dominate the center of this sculpture.

A brown and white sign posted in the field reads: "Navy and Marine/Memorial/DEDICATED TO AMERICANS/LOST AT

SEA," while an escutcheon on the granite base bears the following inscription:

> TO THE STRONG SOULS AND READY VALOR OF THOSE MEN OF THE UNITED STATES WHO IN THE NAVY THE MERCHANT MARINE AND OTHER PATHS OF ACTIVITY UPON THE WATERS OF THE WORLD HAVE GIVEN LIFE OR STILL OFFER IT IN THE PERFORMANCE OF HEROIC DEEDS THIS MONUMENT IS DEDICATED BY A GRATEFUL PEOPLE.

The Navy-Marine Memorial, dedicated October 18, 1934, was installed at a cost of just under $400,000.

Location: Lady Bird Johnson Park, adjacent to George Washington Memorial Parkway.

Ernesto del Piatta's aluminum sculpture pays tribute to the nearly 3,000 sailors and Marines killed in action during World War I. *Photos by Maureen R. Quinn.*

Theodore Roosevelt

An escutcheon on the granite base bears a memorial inscription.
Photo by Maureen R. Quinn.

Teddy Roosevelt was a man of action, so it was particularly ironic that his memorial was concealed from an eager American public for a full year before President Lyndon B. Johnson unveiled the statue. Incarcerated in a wooden crate while pending landscaping issues were resolved, the seventeen-foot heroic bronze of the twenty-sixth president was finally "unleashed" – to paraphrase Secretary of the Interior Stewart L. Udall – on October 27, 1967 (Clopton).

Roosevelt is depicted in a pose that he typically adopted during speeches, with his right hand raised high above his head, and his left hand extended a foot or so from his side. A thirty-foot granite shaft rises behind him. His name is inscribed on the pedestal beneath him, and a plaza in front of him features four granite shafts inscribed with quotations. The cost of the memorial was approximately $1.4 million.

Prior to the addition of sculptor Paul Manship's statue, the entire ninety-one-acre island in the Potomac River was officially the Theodore Roosevelt Memorial. The island is one big nature preserve, and vehicular traffic is prohibited.

Udall presided at the brief dedication ceremony, and his address was followed by speeches from Johnson and Chief Supreme Court Justice Earl Warren. Seated next to President Johnson was Roosevelt's daughter and oldest of five children, Alice Longworth. An often-repeated anecdote involves Roosevelt and a rambunctious young Alice, who was running around her father's office one day when a visitor called on the president. Asked if he intended to discipline the unruly child, Roosevelt supposedly replied, "I can control the country, or Alice, but not both." His most-quoted quote, however, is "Speak softly and carry a big stick."

Johnson said that Roosevelt, a lover of nature and the outdoors, would have approved of the site of his memorial. Then unable to resist a thinly-veiled jab at his political detractors, Johnson implied that Roosevelt might have supported the controversial war in Vietnam.

Johnson also used the occasion to award the Theodore Roosevelt Achievement Medal to NAACP head Roy Wilkins, physicist Arthur Kantrowitz, and physician William B. Walsh (ibid).

Theodore Roosevelt was the fifth cousin of thirty-second president, Franklin Delano Roosevelt. A hero of the Spanish-American War, Lieutenant Colonel Theodore Roosevelt led his "Rough Riders" at San Juan Hill in 1898. He faced numerous personal struggles, which included childhood bouts of ill health, the death of his first wife, Alice, in 1884, and of his youngest son, Quentin, during World War I. He later was elected governor of his native New York, and as William McKinley's vice president, took over as the youngest president after the former's assassination in September of 1901. Roosevelt was forty-two. In 1904, he was elected to a second term. Among Roosevelt's accomplishments were his trust-busting, which prevented a railroad monopoly, his dedication to the conservation of wildlife, and his initiative in the construction of the Panama Canal. He died in 1919, at the age of sixty.

Location: Theodore Roosevelt Island, in the Potomac River.

Photo by Maureen R. Quinn.

Paul Manship's seventeen-foot bronze of Theodore Roosevelt depicts a lion of a man and a legendary president. *Photo by Maureen R. Quinn.*

One of four granite shafts inscribed with quotations from Theodore Roosevelt. *Photo by Maureen R. Quinn.*

A fountain near the plaza of the
Theodore Roosevelt Memorial.
Photos by Maureen R. Quinn.

Tomb of the Unknowns

A solemn ceremony in which the living are honored by being delegated to honor the dead was first observed at Châlons-sur-Marne, France in 1921. Sergeant Edward F. Younger, a decorated World War I veteran, chose from four unmarked coffins a fallen American serviceman to be interred in the newly designated Tomb of the Unknown Soldier at Arlington National Cemetery. The four servicemen had been exhumed from French cemeteries and placed in the city hall. After careful consideration, Younger made his selection by placing a bouquet of roses on one of the caskets. The anonymous serviceman's remains were transported by ship from France to the United States, and buried with full military honors at Arlington National Cemetery. Soil from French battlefields was placed inside the steel vault that enclosed the casket. The three remaining bodies were re-interred in France. Two similar ceremonies followed, in 1956 and 1984. The former combined the selection and re-interment of two World War II casualties —one each from the Pacific and European theaters-and an unknown soldier from the Korean War.

In 1998, the last soldier placed in the Tomb of the Unknowns was exhumed and identified through DNA testing as twenty-three-year old Air Force Lieutenant Michael Joseph Blassie, whose plane was shot down over An Loc, Vietnam in 1972. At the request of his family, Blassie was re-interred at Jefferson Barracks National Cemetery in Saint Louis, Missouri. There is currently no one resting in the Vietnam crypt at the Tomb of the Unknowns (Arlington National Cemetery).

One of the most famous gravesites in Arlington National Cemetery is the Tomb of the Unknowns, constructed in 1921 for an anonymous World War I casualty. Soldiers from World War II, the Korean War, and the Vietnam War were later interred there as well, but the latter was exhumed and buried in another cemetery in 1988 at the request of his family. *Photos by Maureen R. Quinn.*

The Tomb of the Unknowns is located behind the cemetery's white marble Memorial Amphitheater, which was completed in 1920. Sculpted by Thomas Hudson Jones, a nine-foot by eleven-foot by sixteen-foot sarcophagus bears the inscription "Here rests in honored glory an American soldier known but to God." Six bas-relief memorial wreaths, each representing a World War I campaign, are carved on the sides. Since it was originally intended for the World War I soldier, the fifty-ton sarcophagus sits directly atop his grave.

A bas-relief on the side depicts three Classical figures, representing America, Victory, and Peace. Peace stands in between America and Victory, grasping the former's hand and handing the latter a palm branch. A dove is perched on the shield of America.

The Tomb of the Unknowns has a twenty-four-hour honor guard from the Third Infantry.

Location: Behind the Memorial Amphitheater in Arlington National Cemetery, Arlington, Virginia.

4

Further Afield

Adams Memorial

Sculptor Augustus Saint-Gaudens created this memorial in 1891 for the writer Henry Adams (1838-1918), in memory of Adams's wife, Marian, who went by the name "Clover." The cost of the project was $20,000. An equestrian and amateur photographer, the forty-two-year-old Clover poisoned herself in 1885 by drinking chemicals used for developing film. Mental illness, particularly depression, was prevalent in Clover's family. Her Aunt Susan killed herself when Clover was a child, and two years after Clover's death, her sister Ellen committed suicide and their brother Edward attempted to do so, although this tragic chain of events was ostensibly precipitated by the death of Ellen's husband (Krinsley).

Located in Rock Creek Cemetery, the memorial consists of a black, hooded figure, cast in bronze, seated on a rock atop a granite base attached to a large, rectangular headstone. The figure's right hand rests thoughtfully on its chin. Saint-Gaudens did not intend the mysterious figure to be Clover, as many have mistakenly assumed, rather an androgynous, allegorical representation of humanity, meditating on the hereafter. A bench allows visitors to sit and contemplate the statue's meaning, which thousands have done over the past 114 years. The memorial provides no clue to the identity of the deceased, in accordance with Henry's wishes. After his death in 1918, Henry was interred there alongside Clover.

Henry was the grandson of sixth president John Quincy Adams (1767-1848), and the great grandson of second president John Adams (1735-1826). The relationship between Henry and Clover was an odd one. Shortly before their marriage in 1872, Henry confided in a letter to a friend that he did not find Clover particularly attractive. Henry also maintained a lengthy correspondence with a married woman, Elizabeth Cameron, which began a few years before Clover's death and continued for the rest of Henry's life. Following Clover's untimely demise, Henry rarely spoke of his late wife, and destroyed all of the photographs he had of her (ibid). Even his seminal autobiography, *The Education of Henry Adams*, published shortly after his death, makes no direct mention of her.

Two reproductions of the Adams Memorial exist, one at The Saint-Gaudens Memorial Association in Cornish, New Hampshire, and the other in the courtyard of the U.S Court of Appeals for the Federal Circuit, adjacent to Lafayette Park, in Washington, D.C.

Location: Rock Creek Cemetery, Rock Creek Church Road and Webster Street, NW, in Rock Creek Park.

The Adams Memorial, in Rock Creek Cemetery. *Photos by Janet L. Greentree.*

African American Civil War Memorial

The fact that blacks were prohibited from serving in the United States Army may well have prolonged the bloodiest war that the nation ever fought. Prominent abolitionists – among them Frederick Douglass – had from the onset urged President Lincoln to authorize the enlistment of black troops. Nearly two years into the conflict, the Emancipation Proclamation finally cleared the way. Conversely, there had never been any prohibition on blacks enlisting in the navy, and some 20,000 did.

Formed in January of 1863, the 54th Massachusetts Volunteer Infantry was the Union's first black regiment. After a series of skirmishes with Confederate troops, the 700-man unit launched a brave, but unsuccessful assault on Fort Wagner, South Carolina, in July of 1863. Nearly half of the regiment perished along with their commander, Colonel Robert Gould Shaw. Still, their valor convinced Congress to at last authorize the creation of the United States Colored Troops (USCT), prompting a huge wave of black enlistment. The USCT saw action in many major battles, and proved to their detractors the courage and resolution of black soldiers. Abraham Lincoln credited them with turning the tide of the war.

An initiative by Washington, D.C. Councilman Frank Smith led to President George H.W. Bush's signing a law authorizing the creation of a memorial honoring black Civil War veterans. Designed by Louisville, Kentucky, artist Ed Hamilton, the Spirit of Freedom is an eight-foot by nine-foot bronze sculpture that sits atop a rounded, two-foot high pedestal in the center of a granite plaza. Emerging from an amorphous shaft are three black Civil War soldiers and one sailor, who range in age from a fresh-faced recruit at the onset of manhood, to a bearded, middle-aged type. The soldiers assume broad, defensive stances, and are firmly gripping their rifles. The young sailor stands to the right of the bearded soldier, his gaze fixed straight ahead as he steers the half of a ship's wheel that protrudes from the shaft behind him. Etched into the background is a shrouded figure in repose, its large hands crossed peacefully beneath its slumbering countenance. On the opposite side are soldiers' family members bidding them farewell. Encircling the plaza is the Wall of Honor, which has an opening for visitors to step inside. Attached to the wall are 166 stainless steel panels with the names of the 209,145 members of the United States Colored Troops (USCT), as well as the names of their 7,000 white officers, arranged according to regiment. Hamilton's design was selected in 1993 by the African American Civil War Committee. The memorial was dedicated in 1998.

The end of slavery and the inclusion of blacks in the northern army did not end a double standard that persisted for generations. Despite their valiant service, blacks were excluded from the Union's triumphant review of the troops as they marched through the center of Washington, D.C. after the war ended (African American Civil War Memorial Freedom Foundation).

Location: 10th and U streets, N.W.

The African American Civil War Memorial, sculpted by Ed Hamilton of Kentucky, pays tribute to black soldiers who fought for the Union. *Photos by Janet L. Greentree.*

Daniel Webster

The twelve-foot bronze statue of New Hampshire attorney Daniel Webster (1782-1852) stands atop an eighteen-foot pedestal at Massachusetts Avenue and 16th Street, where he looks down at passers-by in Scott Circle. The caped figure's right foot is slightly forward, and his right hand is holding a book, which rests atop an urn-shaped stand. In the center of the pedestal, on the front and back, are bronze reliefs showing historic events in the life of the accomplished orator and politician. On the front, above Webster's name, he is shown during an 1830 session of Congress debating South Carolina Senator Robert Young Hayne over the issue of secession. Above the bronze panel are the words "Liberty and Union, Now and Forever, One and Inseparable." The opposite side shows Webster speaking at the dedication of the Bunker Hill memorial in Boston in 1843. The accompanying inscription reads "Our country, our whole country, and nothing but our country."

Stilson Hutchins, who founded the *Washington Post* in 1877, funded this memorial to his fellow New Hampshire native, and spoke at the 1900 dedication. In his youth, Hutchins had the pleasure of meeting Webster, whom he grew to idolize. Hutchins personally selected Gaetano Trentanove to sculpt the statue, which was created in Trentanove's studio in Florence, Italy. Congress appropriated $4,000 for the granite pedestal.

The dedication ceremonies were held at the Lafayette Square Opera House, after which the entourage of dignitaries and others adjourned to Scott Circle for the unveiling. Among those present were President William McKinley and his cabinet, the justices of the Supreme Court, and several senators and representatives who were members of the Congressional Committee on Arrangements for the Webster memorial.

The speakers were hyperbolic in their praise of Webster, and the one of the few hints that the late statesman and orator had any flaws whatsoever was dropped by New Hampshire senator William E. Chandler, who alluded to Webster's willingness to compromise on the issue of slavery. Chandler was referring specifically to Webster's support of Kentucky Senator Henry Clay's 1850 proposal, which in part, allowed the new states of Arizona, Nevada, New Mexico, and Utah to decide for themselves whether to allow slavery.

Massachusetts senator Henry Cabot Lodge delivered the keynote address, which focused on Webster's unwavering dedication to the preservation of the Union. Although Webster died eight years before the outbreak of the Civil War, Lodge maintained that Webster "was heard again in the deep roar of the Union guns from Sumter to Appomattox."

Webster's great-grandson, Jerome Bonaparte, was given the honor of unveiling the statue.

Stilson Hutchins, who founded the *Washington Post* in 1877, funded this memorial to his fellow New Hampshire native, Daniel Webster. *Photo by Maureen R. Quinn.*

Webster served in Congress for over two decades, and went on to become Secretary of State. His most famous legal case was one that never actually occurred, one in which he defends a man who has sold his soul to the Devil. At the conclusion of Stephen Vincent Benet's short story, the triumphant Webster successfully exonerates his client from eternal damnation, then sends Old Nick off with an arm-twisting and a sharp kick in the backside.

Location: Massachusetts Avenue and 16th Street, in Scott Circle.

On the front of the pedestal, a bronze bas-relief depicts Webster during an 1830 session of Congress, debating South Carolina Senator Robert Young Hayne over the issue of secession. *Photos by Maureen R. Quinn.*

Dante Alighieri

Washington, D.C. seems an odd location for a twelve-foot bronze statue of the Father of Italian poetry. The stern figure of Dante, holding a volume of his *Commedia*, is perched atop a square granite pedestal in Meridian Hill Park. With his long robe and laurel garland, Dante might easily be mistaken for an ancient Roman scribe, if not for the name chiseled beneath him. The memorial was erected in 1921 by Carlo Barsotti, a New York City newspaper publisher, to commemorate the 600th anniversary of Dante's death. The sculptor was Ximemes Ettore.

Dante Alighieri's epic *Commedia*, known as *The Divine Comedy*, bears a haunting similarity to the peripatetic existence that characterized the last two decades in the life of Italy's premier poet. Banished from his native Florence by a political faction that seized power in 1302, Dante was forced to spend the remainder of his days wandering from city to city, seeking out the protection and patronage of the rich and powerful. In the person of Guido Novello da Polenta, Dante found a somewhat avuncular figure, and was able to live out the remainder of his days in relative peace in the latter's home in Ravenna. Dante died in 1321, at the age of fifty-six.

Dark and mysterious, the stern bronze figure of Dante dominates a small square in Meridian Hill Park. *Photos by Maureen R. Quinn.*

With the Roman poet Virgil at his side, the narrator of *The Divine Comedy* goes on an allegorical journey, during which he witnesses first hand the terrible punishments of Hell, and the excruciations endured by those in Purgatory. Because Virgil is a pagan, however, he is unable to escort Dante to Paradise, so that task is left to Beatrice. Dante based her character on that of Beatrice Portinari, whom he had loved since first setting eyes on her when he was nine years old. Both Dante and Beatrice, who died in 1290, married other people. Beatrice appears in *La Vita Nuova*, Dante's first great work.

Dante's *Commedia* is rife with figures from both the annals of history and mythology, and in many ways set the standard for depictions of the afterlife. He even challenged the long-held belief that Perdition is one gigantic inferno, and the worst sinners in *Commedia* must endure an eternity of freezing cold. Dante seems to have posthumously deflected criticism that he relegated his political foes to the various circles of Hell, and his *Commedia* raised awareness of long-standing social ills.

Location: Florida Avenue and 16th Street, in Meridian Hill Park.

Edmund Burke

The statue of Edmund Burke is somewhat of an anomaly in Washington, D.C., as he is the only British subject memorialized for his contributions to the cause of American independence.

Although the Irish-born statesman and orator did not advocate secession of the Colonies, he stated his opposition to the 1765 Stamp Act, and believed that England was too harsh in many of her policies toward America. Through his speeches and writings, Burke unsuccessfully tried to mitigate the growing hostilities, which eventually culminated in the American Revolution. Burke's sympathy toward America, tempered nonetheless by his loyalty to the Crown, probably served to increase the Colonists' resolve. As a member of Parliament, Burke advocated strongly for greater scrutiny of royal expenditures, and supported increased limitations on the power of the monarchy.

Though expressed with eloquent rhetoric and sincere passion, Burke's positions were often inconsistent, vacillating between progressive and conservative. He advocated fairer treatment of both the American colonies and Catholics in England, yet fervently opposed the French Revolution and in later writings, argued against freedom of speech in certain matters. His 1790 treatise *Reflections on the Revolution in France* caused not a little discord among some of his former political supporters (Kreis).

The eight-foot bronze figure that stands at Massachusetts Avenue and 11th Street, N.W. depicts Burke waving his right hand, as if greeting someone. The inscription beneath on the granite pedestal reads: "BURKE/1729-1797/MAGNANIMITY/ IN POLITICS IS/NOT SELDOM THE/TRUEST WISDOM."

Sculpted by J. Harvard Thomas, the statue is a reproduction of an original located in Bristol, England. At the 1922 dedication, former London mayor Sir Charles Wakefield presented the memorial to the city of Washington, D.C. (Goode: 277).

Perched atop his granite pedestal, an eight-foot Edmund Burke waves to passers-by. *Photos by Maureen R. Quinn.*

The project was funded by the Sulgrave Institution, an organization founded to foster good relations between the United States and Great Britain. The organization now maintains Sulgrave Manor, which was built in 1500 by Lawrence Washington, an ancestor of the first American president.

Location: Massachusetts Avenue and 11th Street, N.W.

Emancipation Monument

The years following the assassination of Abraham Lincoln were marked by a mixture of bereavement, gratitude, and reverence to the man credited with saving the Union and ensuring the freedom of three million people. Ten years after the first public monument commemorating the sixteenth president was erected at C and 4th streets, in Judiciary Square, a second memorial to the enduring emancipator was placed at East Capitol Avenue and 12th Street, in what was then Lincoln Square. This bronze sculpture depicts the sixteenth president granting freedom to a kneeling slave. The latter is based on a photograph taken of Archer Alexander, who was the last slave to be captured under the Fugitive Slave Act. The statue of Lincoln is twelve feet in height, as is the granite pedestal which supports the figures of him and Alexander. Lincoln's right hand holds a furled copy of the January 1, 1863 Emancipation Proclamation, which rests atop a podium. Alexander – clad in a loincloth and wearing broken manacles on his wrists – kneels patiently beneath the president's extended left hand. Below the two figures is the word "EMANCIPATION." American sculptor Thomas Ball created the piece in his studio in Florence, Italy. Ball was the son of a Boston sign painter, and his work in the family business led him to undertake portrait painting, then finally sculpture (Taft: 142).

The dedication took place on a rainy April 14, 1876, the eleventh anniversary of Lincoln's death, and drew a crowd of 50,000, many freed slaves. Also in attendance were President Ulysses S. Grant and his cabinet, as well as members of the Supreme Court. Abolitionist Frederick Douglass was the keynote speaker. The eloquent Douglass did

not deliver the eulogy to the slain president that most of the crowd expected, implying that Lincoln's motives were not entirely ingenuous, and that he had done too little too late (Jacob: 25).

The 1876 Emancipation Monument by Thomas Ball is one of several "Lincoln Memorials" in the capital. *Photos by Janet L. Greentree.*

The $18,000 for the monument was donated by former slaves, while Congress footed the $3,000 bill for the granite pedestal. Charlotte Scott, herself a former slave, proposed the idea for the memorial, and even donated the first five dollars that she earned as a freewoman.

Location: East Capitol Avenue and 12th Street, in Lincoln Park.

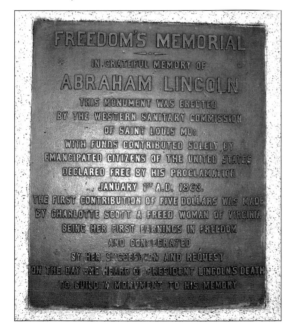

A bronze memorial plaque on the Emancipation Monument. *Photo by Janet L. Greentree.*

George B. McClellan

Major General George B. McClellan sits erect in his saddle, clad in his full uniform, his sheathed saber dangling at his left side. His mount taps the ground impatiently with its hoof. On either side of the oblong pedestal that supports the nine-foot sculpture is an elaborate bronze relief depicting an array of armaments – spears, axes, eagle-capped staffs, and a pair of crossed cannons – draped in shrouds and laurel wreaths. A protruding pile of cannon balls is visible at the bottom. Encircling the base of the pedestal is a bronze laurel garland, clamped in the beaks of four eagles, who sit on all corners. President Theodore Roosevelt was the guest of honor at the statue's May 2, 1907 dedication. The statue of McClellan is one of several in Dupont Circle.

Frederick MacMonnies began work on the piece in 1905, three years after his design had been selected from among twenty-eight others in 1902 by a panel of distinguished sculptors and architects. Under the tutelage of Augustus Saint-Gaudens, MacMonnies had evolved into a prominent artist. The high point of his career was his creation of the Triumph of Columbia fountain for the 1893 World Fair in Chicago.

Nicknamed "Little Mac," McClellan was a West Point graduate who fought in two wars, and served a term as governor of New Jersey shortly before his death in 1885. He lost the 1864 presidential election to incumbent Republican Abraham Lincoln. McClellan was given command of the Army of the Potomac shortly after the Union's defeat at the First Battle of Bull Run, but the position was short-lived. In 1862, he faced growing criticism from President Lincoln and members of his cabinet for procrastinating, and not moving aggressively enough against the Confederacy. McClellan was eventually replaced by Ambrose Burnside, who was in turn replaced by Joseph Hooker, who himself was replaced by Winfield Scott Hancock. In letters to his wife, Mary Ellen, McClellan expressed contempt for Lincoln. McClellan's son, George, Jr., served two terms as mayor of New York City.

Location: Connecticut Avenue and Columbia Road, N.W., in Dupont Circle.

Major General George B. McClellan, sculpted by Frederick MacMonnies. *Photo courtesy of Bull Run Civil War Round Table.*

George H. Thomas

On a windy September day in 1863, Major General George H. Thomas sat on his horse atop Snodgrass Hill, defiantly staring down at the menacing Army of Tennessee gathered below him. Much of the Union forces under Major General William S. Rosencrans had already scattered, beaten back by repeated Confederate assaults. Like Stonewall Jackson two years earlier at First Bull Run, Thomas stood cool and confident in the face of danger. But unlike Jackson, who was able to hold out against an encroaching enemy until reinforcements arrived, Thomas's stand at Chickamagua Creek in Georgia did not end in a victory for his side. He was finally forced to withdraw, ceding his position to Confederate General Braxton Bragg. But his courage and tenacity did manage to avoid a complete rout by the South, and earned him command of the Army of the Cumberland and the moniker "the Rock of Chickamauga." The remaining Federal troops returned to the city of Chattanooga, Tennessee, which they had recently captured. Although the engagement officially ended in a Confederate victory, Southern forces suffered slightly more casualties, about 18,000 to the North's 16,000. In the 1890s, the site of the battle was made into a national military park.

The bronze sculpture of Major General George H. Thomas was the fifth memorial in Washington, D.C. honoring a Civil War general, and the third equestrian statue to do so. Erected in 1879, the fourteen-foot statue depicts the bearded Thomas sitting calmly with his hat in his right hand, while his left hand grips the reins. His horse stands erect against a strong wind, its front hooves resting on a rock, its mouth open in a silent whinny. The faded inscription on one side of the statue's pedestal reads "MAJ. GEN. GEORGE H. THOMAS./SAN FRANCISCO CAL./ MARCH 28, 1870," the latter referring to his date of death. The inscription on the opposite side reads "ERECTED BY HIS COMRADES/OF THE SOCIETY OF/ THE ARMY OF THE CUMBERLAND." The piece was cast from old Civil War cannons.

Major General George H. Thomas, as he might have looked at Chickamauga Creek in September of 1863. *Photo courtesy of Bull Run Civil War Round Table.*

The work was New York sculptor John Quincy Adams Ward's first commission for an equestrian statue, and was praised for its bold, dramatic style, while criticized by some for minor imperfections. Ward spend five years on the Thomas Memorial, and was paid $35,000. He had gained some notoriety in 1870 with the unveiling of his Shakespeare sculpture for New York City's Central Park. In 1874, Ward had been elected president of the National Academy of Design.

The November 19, 1879 dedication was preceded by a huge parade. The press was delighted with the gala event. Among those in attendance were President Rutherford B. Hayes and his wife, Lucy, as well as former fellow generals of the late Thomas, one of whom gave the dedication speech.

Location: Massachusetts Avenue and 14th Street N.W., in Thomas Circle.

Henry Wadsworth Longfellow

Before its gradual deterioration into the rambling, non-rhythmic, stream-of-consciousness that today characterizes this once great art form, poetry enjoyed a national revival in the likes of figures such as Henry Wadsworth Longfellow (1807-1882). The son of an influential New England attorney, Longfellow imbued his writing with pathos, imagery, and lyricism that transcended social strata. At one time, every school child was familiar with his epics "Hiawatha" and "Evangeline." A strict adherent to traditional meter and rhyme, Longfellow would probably be condemned by modern critics for penning "sing-song" verses.

Following a seven-year professorship at his alma mater, Bowdoin College in Maine, Longfellow taught language and European literature at Harvard University from 1836 to 1854, after which he resigned. Although Longfellow's life was a long, successful, prolific one, it was marred by personal tragedy. He was married and widowed twice, his first wife's dying in childbirth and his second wife from burns received in a fire. Longfellow died in Cambridge, Massachusetts, about a month after his seventy-fifth birthday.

In 1909, he was immortalized in bronze as perhaps he would have wanted to be depicted, in a pensive, if somewhat somber pose. He sits in his chair on a multi-tiered, pink granite pedestal in Dupont Circle, surrounded by vehicular and pedestrian traffic, and oblivious to the occasional insults inflicted by visiting pigeons. His chin is resting on his right hand, and he is holding a book under his left arm. The statue was erected by the Longfellow Memorial Association.

The 700 chairs that were set up were insufficient for the crowd that turned out for the May 8, 1909 dedication. On the platform with the speakers were Longfellow's two daughters, six granddaughters, two grandsons, and a niece. On the front of the speaker's podium were lines from Longfellow's poem "Sail On, O Ship of State." Erica Thorpe, the poet's youngest grandchild, unveiled the memorial.

What might have been a long, elaborate ceremony was cut short by an unexpected rain, prompting the attorney general, standing in for President William Howard Taft, to condense his speech to "I represent the President, and for him, in behalf of the United States Government, I accept this statue." Afterward, someone joked that Longfellow had been baptized as well as unveiled (*Washington Post*).

The Longfellow memorial was sculpted by Thomas Ball, who was ninety at the time, and his son-in-law, William Couper. Ball, who also sculpted the Emancipation Monument in Lincoln Park, took the young Daniel Chester French under his wing in 1875. French studied at Ball's studio in Florence, Italy until 1877.

Location: Connecticut Avenue and M Street, N.W., in Dupont Circle.

James Buchanan

The facial expression of the eight-foot sculpture of James Buchanan in Meridian Hill Park hints at his inglorious presidency. The term of the fifteenth president (1857-1861) was marred by growing dissent between the northern and southern states, and Buchanan has been blamed for leaving an utter mess for Abraham Lincoln to sort out. Critics have implied that he was too complacent, trusting that an increasingly divisive situation would somehow resolve itself. Cast in bronze, Buchanan is seated in front of a marble column flanked by symbolic granite figures representing Law and Diplomacy. The president's eyes are cast downwards diffidently, ostensibly reading the newspaper in his lap, but perhaps avoiding the gaze of spectators. The memorial was sculpted by Hans Shuler, and designed by William Gordon Beecher.

Harriet Lane Johnson funded this $100,000 memorial to her uncle, fifteenth president James Buchanan. *Photos by Janet L. Greentree.*

Understandably, Herbert Hoover could sympathize with Buchanan. Hoover's term coincided with one of the worst crises that the nation had ever faced – the Great Depression – for which he was almost entirely blamed. In dedicating the Buchanan memorial on June 26, 1930, Hoover focused on Buchanan's political successes, which he argued far outweighed his shortcomings. Buchanan, Hoover recalled, had served admirably as a senator, ambassador to Great Britain, and Secretary of State. Although he never married and had no children of his own, Hoover added, Buchanan was like a father to his orphaned niece,

Harriet Lane Johnson, whose will had provided for $100,000 for the erection of a memorial to her uncle.

Buchanan's failures, Hoover allowed, were due to circumstance rather than incompetence. Buchanan had the misfortune to be elected president "when no human power could have stayed the inexorable advance of a great national conflict." Then waxing metaphorical, Hoover compared the Civil War to a terrible storm which had engulfed the country.

Location: Florida Avenue and 16th Street, Meridian Hill Park.

Joan of Arc

The patron saint of France is the only woman to be memorialized in an equestrian statue in Washington, D.C. The statue of Joan of Arc was erected in 1922 by the Société de Femmes de France (Society of French Women) of New York, and was presented as a gift from the women of France to the women of the United States. The legendary savior of France is galloping into battle, clad in full plate armor and brandishing a long sword in her right hand. Her bronze steed is delicately balanced on the pedestal, with its right front and left rear hooves in the air. The statue is a replica of an original sculpted by Paul DuBois for Rheims Cathedral in France.

Joan of Arc, the patron saint of France, was erected in 1922 by the Société de Femmes de France (Society of French Women) of New York and presented as a gift from the women of France to the women of the United States. *Photos by Janet L. Greentree.*

A simple peasant girl, Joan was born in 1421 in Domremy, France, in the province of Champagne. Her parents were farmers. When she was thirteen, she believed that she had been chosen by God to save her country from the English, who had occupied much of France during the Hundred Years War. She maintained that she had been apprised of her divine mission by various saints, who manifested themselves through voices and flashes of light. She led French troops to victory in 1429, ousting the English from the city of Orleans, but was later captured by the Burgundians, who were in league with the enemies of French king Charles VII. After being sold to the English, she was eventually convicted of witchcraft and heresy, and burned at the stake in Rouen, France, in 1431. Charles VII, who owed his crown to the nineteen-year-old heroine, did virtually nothing to secure her release. Among Joan's "crimes" was the fact that she broke convention by wearing men's clothing and leading soldiers into battle. She was canonized in 1920.

Location: Florida Avenue and 16th Street, in Meridian Hill Park.

John A. Logan

Honoring the wishes of Mrs. Mary Logan, The Logan Memorial Commission chose sculptor Franklin Simmons, who had created the Peace Memorial for Admiral David Porter, to craft a fitting tribute to the late major general. Simmons completed the bronze sculpture at his studio in Florence, Italy in 1901, and the dedication was held April 9 of that year in Washington, D.C.'s Iowa Circle, later renamed Logan Circle. Simmons received $65,000 for his work. About ten percent of the monument's cost was raised by private donors, while Congress appropriated the remainder.

Bas-relief panels on the base of this equestrian statue show scenes contrasting Logan's military and political life. The front panel – on the pedestal's northern face – depicts the allegorical figure of war. Opposite her – on the rear of the pedestal – stands Peace. The eastern panel shows Logan and his fellow generals gathered in conference. Beneath them, on the pedestal's first tier, is the inscription "LOGAN." The western panel shows Logan being sworn in as senator in 1879, but is full of historical inaccuracies (Jacob: 84). Fluted columns on the corners of the pedestal frame the four scenes. The entire monument is bronze.

From the base of the pedestal to the top of the general's wide-brimmed hat measures about twenty-five feet. Logan's sword is drawn, resting for the moment at his side. His expression is sharp and alert, his noble visage decked with his large, drooping mustache. The horse is poised and majestic, its right front hoof raised a foot or so above the ground, as if just beginning a gallop.

Pigeons perch atop the hat of Major General John A. Logan, in Logan Circle, Vermont Avenue at 13th and P Streets N.W. The pedestal's western side has a bronze bas-relief that depicts Logan's being sworn in as senator in 1879. *Photo courtesy of Bull Run Civil War Round Table.*

Major General John A. Logan served in both the Mexican and Civil wars, and fought at the First Battle of Bull Run in 1861. After James B. McPherson was killed by Confederate troops in Atlanta in July of 1864, Logan briefly assumed command of the Army of the Tennessee.

Logan was a charter member of both the Grand Army of the Republic (see previous entry, p.___) **(*Please complete at layout. Thanks.)** and the Society of the Army of the Tennessee, the latter which commissioned his official monument in 1886. While serving as Commander-in-Chief of the GAR in 1868, Logan established May 30 as a day for all posts to remember soldiers killed in battle. This set the stage for the first Memorial Day – then called Decoration Day. After his military service, Logan enjoyed a long career in politics, serving as a congressman and then senator for Illinois. He was Republican candidate James G. Blaine's running mate in the 1884 presidential election, but the pair lost to Democrats Grover Cleveland and Thomas Hendricks. Logan died two years later, while serving his third term as senator.

Location: Vermont Avenue at 13th and P Streets N.W., in Logan Circle.

John Carroll

At an annual banquet of the National Alumni Society in 1909, Georgetown University professor John A. Conway proposed to fellow alumni a memorial to John Carroll, the first American bishop and the founder of their alma mater. After raising $6,700, a committee appointed by the university's president selected Jerome Conner for the task. Conner, a thirty-seven-year-old Irish immigrant, was a self-taught sculptor who began working as a stone-cutter in New York at the age of thirteen. The committee was familiar and obviously impressed with Conner's bust of Irish poet Thomas Moore in the Corcoran Gallery of Art (*New York Times*).

John Carroll founded Georgetown University in 1789, the same year that he was appointed the Bishop of Baltimore by Pope Pius VI. This memorial, sculpted by Jerome Conner, was unveiled in 1912. *Photos courtesy of Georgetown University.*

Assembled from about fifteen different pieces of bronze, the six-foot statue depicts a seated John Carroll, clad in the garments of a Jesuit priest. The inscription at the base reads "JOHN CARROLL/FOUNDER."

The dedication was held May 4, 1912 during the second day of a three-day reunion of the National Alumni Society. Standing in for President Taft, who could not attend, Attorney General George C. Wickersham gave the keynote address. Following the actual unveiling were remarks by Cardinal Gibbons of Baltimore.

College students have traditionally made the austere statue the butt of their pranks, which have included putting a toilet underneath the chair on which Carroll is seated. To prevent this particularly irreverent joke, the university filled in that area with a sculptural addition of a stack of books in 1934 (Goode: 487). In 1990, extensive restoration work was done on the statue, which had long endured the effects of time, weather, and occasional vandalism.

John Carroll was born in Maryland in 1735. He studied and later taught in Europe, returning to Maryland shortly before the outbreak of the Revolutionary War. His brother Charles was one of the fifty-six signers of the Declaration of Independence. In 1776, he traveled to Canada with Charles, Benjamin Franklin, and Samuel Chase in an attempt to gain support for the revolution. This proved to be of no avail, however. Carroll established Georgetown University in 1789, the year that he was appointed Bishop of Baltimore by Pope Pius VI. Carroll died in 1815 at the age of eighty, and is buried at the Basilica of the Assumption, in Baltimore.

Location: Q and 38th streets, in front of the Healy Building, Healy Circle, Georgetown University Campus.

John Witherspoon

The progenitors of many great ideas and institutions never lived to reap what they had sown. Some knew from the onset that future generations would have that honor, or responsibility, while others fully anticipated that they would have the satisfaction of seeing their lofty dreams become reality. The Founding Fathers, as well as those who gave their lives for the liberty of their country, did not know how America would fare, or whether or not she would even survive the challenges ahead. One of those men was John Witherspoon (1722-1794), a Scottish-born Presbyterian minister who came to America in 1768. Witherspoon served as a delegate to the Continental Congress, and later was president of the College of New Jersey, which became Princeton University. Over a century after Witherspoon's death, Teunis S. Hamlin decided to erect a statue to this signer of the Declaration of Independence, in front of the Church of the Covenant at N Street and Connecticut Avenue, where Hamlin was pastor. Regrettably, Hamlin did not live to see his dream become reality, either, but Vice President James S. Sherman said prior to the unveiling that the attendees who had gathered to honor Witherspoon were, in effect, honoring Hamlin, too.

Thomas Ball's ten-foot heroic bronze of Reverend John Witherspoon (1722-1794), Presbyterian minister and one of the fifty-six signers of the Declaration of Independence. *Photos by Maureen R. Quinn*.

Well in advance of the May 20, 1909 dedication, the Witherspoon Memorial Association sent invitations to as many of Witherspoon's descendants as they could find, and a huge number turned out. Among them were two of Witherspoon's granddaughters, the reverends Jeremiah Witherspoon and David W. Woods – who delivered the invocation and benediction, respectively – and young William Banks Withers, who was given the honor of unveiling the statue.

The speakers that day, while acknowledging Witherspoon's support of the Revolution, did not go into specifics so much as they praised the general aspects of his character. Ambassador from Great Britain James Bryce summarized the contributions of his fellow Scotsman, calling him "a remarkable man in all his three characters, as pastor, politician, and college president." Other speakers that day included former Secretary of State John Foster, future United States president Woodrow Wilson – who at the time was president of Princeton University – and one of the commissioners of the District of Columbia.

Thomas Ball's ten-foot heroic bronze of Witherspoon shows the minister standing tall, the Bible tucked neatly under his right arm. On all four side of the pedestal are inscribed bronze plaques. The plaque on the pedestal's front, or south side, bears a relief of a laurel garland, in whose center are Witherspoon's name and life dates. The opposite plaque contains a lengthy quote alluding to Witherspoon's signing of the Declaration of Independence:

> For my own part, of property I have some, of reputa-
> tion more. That reputation is staked, that property is

pledged on the issue of this contest: and although these gray hairs must soon descend into the sepulcher, I would immediately rather that they descend thither by the hand of the executioner than desert at this crisis the sacred cause of my country.

The Witherspoon memorial was funded mostly by private donations, although Congress appropriated $4,000 for the granite pedestal.

Location: In front of the Church of the Covenant, N Street and Connecticut Avenue, in Dupont Circle.

Lieutenant General George Washington

American morale reached a low point late in 1776, a year and a half after the unofficial start of the war of independence. The rebels had won no victories, confidence in the army's leadership was flagging, and desertion was as much of an epidemic as the bouts of dysentery and typhoid that ravaged the camps. General George Washington knew that he had one last chance to save the revolution.

A force of Hessian mercenaries under Colonel Johann Rall was camped at Trenton, New Jersey, across the Delaware River from 2,500 American troops. The Hessians were aware of the Americans, but did not consider them a serious threat. Complacent and condescending, the Hessians spent Christmas Eve feasting and carousing. In the meantime, Washington and his men began crossing the frigid Delaware on wooden rafts, breaking up the ice floes that covered the surface of the river. Groggy from a night of drunken revelry, the Hessians were caught unprepared. The Americans captured the camp, taking 1,200 prisoners. According to one story, someone had tried to warn Rall the previous evening, handing him a note which told of the Americans' plan. Unconcerned, the colonel stuffed the note into his pocket and returned to his party. Lying mortally wounded the following day, he finally read the note. Another version holds that the folded note was found on the colonel's body the next morning. Whatever the case, he failed to heed the warning.

In 1860, Clark Mills received much acclaim for an equestrian statue of Lieutenant General George Washington. The dramatic pose of horse and rider is supposedly based on a painting of Washington at the Battle of Trenton. The sculptor's superb rendering of Major General Andrew Jackson in Lafayette Park was probably the main factor in his receiving the $50,000 commission for the Washington sculpture.

Mills had originally intended a much more elaborate monument to Washington, but the funds were insufficient to execute these plans. These designs called for the addition of two equestrian sculptures, flanking five standing figures, on a lower tier of a pedestal with a concave front. Below these secondary sculptures would be five relief panels depicting various scenes from the American

Revolution. Only the statue of Washington at the very top remained basically unchanged in the final result (Goode: 384-385).

Lieutenant General George Washington by Clark Mills. Mills supposedly based the sculpture on a painting of Washington at the Battle of Trenton. *Photos by Maureen R. Quinn.*

Sculptor and author Lorado Taft panned much of Mills's work, finding it lacking in inspiration and creativity. He even described the much-vaunted Jackson sculpture as "misconceived" and felt that the general seemed to be "bowing and performing" (228). Still, the accomplishments of Mills are impressive, especially considering that he had no formal training in sculpture, having improvised what he learned as a woodworker and mason. His first moment of glory came when he created a marble bust of John C. Calhoun for the city of Charleston, South Carolina.

Location: Washington Circle, 23rd Street and Pennsylvania Avenue.

Mahatma Gandhi

Lobbying for a memorial for Mahatma Gandhi, India's martyred civil rights leader, picked up speed in 1997, the year that marked the fiftieth anniversary of his country's independence from British rule. The statue was unveiled on September 16, 2000, during an official visit to the United States by Indian Prime Minister Shri Atal Bihari Vajpayee. President William J. Clinton was in attendance. The dedication came nearly two years to the day after Congress unanimously approved the Indian government's request for a monument to Mahatma Gandhi on public land. Gautam Pal, who had created bronze memorials of several other humanitarian icons, won a competition for the design. The landscaping was done by a Virginia architectural firm.

The memorial sits in the northwest corner of a miniature, triangular park formed by the intersection of Q Street, 21st Street, and Massachusetts Avenue. Pedestrian walkways lined with a six-inch curb provide a buffer between the traffic from the three busy thoroughfares. A circular plaza of black granite bricks surrounds the eight and a half foot figure of Gandhi, who is mounted on a nine-foot by seven-foot by three-foot pedestal of roughly-hewn red granite. A five-foot long red granite bench is located on the plaza's western section. Opposite the bench, on the plaza's eastern section, are three gray granite steles supporting panels with inscriptions on them. Beyond the steles is a small copse of trees, among them a 100-year-old weeping beech.

Born in 1869, Gandhi was schooled in England, eventually earning a law degree there. He knew that in spite of his intelligence and educational advantages, he would always be treated as a second-class citizen by the English, who at that time occupied his country. Resolving to rid India of British imperialism, Gandhi threw off all of the false trappings of class and prestige, and began a massive campaign of peaceful protests. Gandhi called civil disobedience ". . .the assertion of a right which law should give, but which it denies." His followers staged marches, and their boycotts of British products severely impacted the English economy. Gandhi's efforts drew the ire of British Prime Minister Winston Churchill, who called him "a half-naked Indian fakir." Repeatedly jailed, Gandhi did not relent, eventually shaking off the yoke of the British in 1947. A year later, the man who had so fervently preached non-violence was shot by a Pakistani Muslim, who was subsequently executed for his crime.

Location: Across the street from the Indian Embassy, Massachusetts Avenue and 21st Street, in Dupont Circle.

This memorial to Indian civil rights leader Mahatma Gandhi was unveiled September 16, 2000. A circular plaza of black granite bricks surrounds the eight-and-a-half-foot figure of Gandhi, who is mounted on a nine-foot by seven-foot by three-foot pedestal of rough-hewn red granite. *Photos by Maureen R. Quinn.*

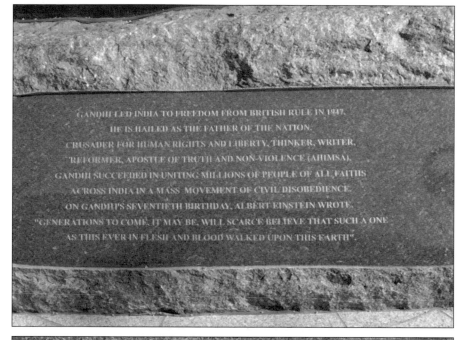

The memorial also features panels inscribed with quotes and biographical information about Gandhi. *Photos by Maureen R. Quinn.*

Martin Luther

This memorial to the father of the Reformation was dedicated on May 21, 1884 by the Martin Luther Society of New York, to commemorate the 400th anniversary of the German preacher's birth. The eleven and a half-foot bronze depicts Luther (1483-1546) in ecclesiastical robes, clutching the Bible, as he appeared before the Imperial Diet of Worms in 1521. The three-ton statue was cast at a foundry in Germany, and shipped by boat to the United States. The original was designed by German sculptor Ernest Rietschel and completed by Adolf Doundorf following Rietschel's death, and is a duplicate of the central figure in an 1868 sculptural group in Worms. The first monument to Martin Luther erected in the United States, the statue was funded by approximately $10,000 in donations. In 1956, the Luther Statue Association had tentative plans to install lighting around the memorial at a cost of roughly $4,000, but this idea was scuttled. Over the next seventy-five years, additional statues of Luther appeared in Streator, Illinois; Saint Paul, Minnesota; Detroit, Michigan; Saint Louis, Missouri; Dubuqe and Decorah, Iowa; Baltimore, Maryland; Gettysburg, Pennsylvania; Springfield, Illinois; and Louisville, Kentucky (De Vries: 16-17). The Gettysburg statue, by Hans Schuler, is the only one depicting a seated Luther. Schuler also sculpted the Baltimore statue.

Luther's father sent him to the University of Erfurt to study law, and was less than supportive of his son's seemingly sudden decision to entertain an ecclesiastical calling. An often-repeated anecdote is that Luther was traveling home one July night in 1502 during a fierce thunderstorm, and was driven to sheer terror by the intensity of the growing tempest. As the searing flashes of lightning edged closer and closer, he beseeched the powers-that-be to spare his life, in return for which he would become a monk.

Luther's fervent, burning piety often reached manic climaxes, and he was as much driven by his terror of the supernatural as by his love of Christ. The superstitious climate in which he lived helped foster his paranoia, and he asserted on many occasions that he had been harassed by the Devil himself.

In his famous Ninety-five Theses, Luther railed against a plethora of corrupt practices which plagued the Catholic Church, including the sale of indulgences, promises by church officials to shorten time spent in Purgatory in exchange for payments by relatives of the deceased, and simony, the sale of so-called relics and church offices. Historians now dispute whether Luther actually nailed his theses to the door of the church in Wittenburg, the consensus being that he simply included them with a letter that he mailed to church officials (KDG Wittenburg). Luther was summoned to Rome to answer charges of heresy, and subsequently excommunicated. At the Diet of Worms the following year, he refused to recant his anti-establishment views, supposedly uttering his famous remark "Here I stand. I cannot do otherwise. God help me! Amen." Fearing for his safety, Luther's supporters whisked him off to Wartburg, where he translated the Bible into German while he was in hiding. Luther's support grew steadily, at one point even inciting riots against church officials. Luther denounced these acts of violence.

Martin Luther, Father of the Reformation. This statue in front of Luther Place Memorial Church in Washington, D.C. is a replica of one that stands in a sculpture group in Worms, Germany. The Washington, D.C. statue was the first memorial erected to Luther in the United States. *Photos by Maureen R. Quinn.*

Although revered for his courageous stance and unwavering devotion to his beliefs, Luther had a dark side. In his younger days, he was tolerant of the Jews, expecting that eventually, they would come to recognize "the true faith." Toward the end of his life, however, Luther became virulently anti-Semitic, in his 1543 book *Against the Jews and Their Lies* calling for the destruction of Jewish homes and businesses, and the expulsion of the non-believers from Germany. His vituperations formed the crux of German anti-Semitism, which culminated in the horrific events some 400 years later.

Location: Luther Place Memorial Church, Massachusetts Avenue and 14th Street, in Thomas Circle.

Mary McLeod Bethune

On the afternoon of July 10, 1974, seventy-five-year-old Albertus McLeod Bethune, Jr. was beaming. A crowd of 20,000 had flocked to the capital's Lincoln Park to pay tribute to his late mother, noted black educator and activist Dr. Mary McLeod Bethune (1875-1955). A memorial was to be unveiled in the presence of thousands of supporters, spectators, dignitaries, and politicians, among them Walter Washington, the first mayor of Washington, D.C. One of several speakers to address the crowd prior to the unveiling, Washington said that although Bethune herself was "larger than life", her goals were realistic

(Hunter). Dorothy Height, president of the National Council of Negro Women, noted in her address that the dedication marked the first monument to both a black person and a woman on public grounds in the capital.

Bethune's ambitions were not deterred by her humble origins, and if anything, the struggles that characterized her early years were the impetus for her later successes. She was born in South Carolina to former slaves, and was the fifteenth of seventeen children. In her youth, she had ambitions of becoming a missionary, but found her calling much closer to home. She dedicated tremendous time and effort to improving the educational and social opportunities for blacks, founding the Daytona Literary and Industrial School for Training Negro Girls. She served for nearly forty years as president of this institution, which later became Bethune-Cookman College. In addition to her career as a teacher and administrator, Bethune served in various capacities throughout the administrations of four different presidents, most notably as head of the National Youth Administration's Division of Negro Affairs under Franklin D. Roosevelt. Bethune developed a close friendship with both Eleanor Roosevelt and President Roosevelt's mother (Fleming). Bethune died in 1955 at the age of seventy-nine, and is buried on the grounds of the college that she founded.

This bronze sculpture group in Lincoln Park depicts Bethune imparting final words of wisdom to a couple of black children, a girl and a boy. In Bethune's right hand she is holding a cane. In her left hand is a furled piece of paper, representing the legacy that she is handing to the young girl standing next to her. The figure of Bethune is seventeen feet tall. Around the six sides of the sculpture's concrete base are inscribed the words:

> I leave you love. I leave you hope. I leave you the challenge of developing confidence in one another. I leave you a thirst for education. I leave you a respect for the use of power. I leave you faith. I leave you racial dignity. I leave you a desire to live harmoniously with your fellow men. I leave you, finally, a responsibility to our young people.

The sculptor was Robert Berks of New York, who also created the bronze bust of John F. Kennedy in the lobby of the Kennedy Center for the Performing Arts. The $400,000 cost of the Bethune memorial was borne by the National Council of Negro Women – which Bethune established in 1935 – and the National Park Service.

Location: East Capitol and 12th streets, in Lincoln Park.

MARY McLEOD BETHUNE
1875   1955
Let her works praise her

Sculpted by Robert Berks, this 1974 memorial to educator Mary McLeod Bethune was the first erected to a woman and a black person on public ground in Washington, D.C. *Photo by Janet L. Greentree.*

Nuns of the Battlefield

Dedicated in 1924, this memorial was sculpted by Jerome Connor, and features a six by nine-foot bronze bas-relief panel depicting twelve Civil War nurses, each nurse representing the different religious orders that cared for sick and wounded soldiers. Represented are Sisters of Saint Joseph, Sisters of Our Lady of Mount Carmel, Sisters of Saint Dominic, Sisters of Saint Ursula, Sisters of the Holy Cross, Sisters of the Poor of Saint Francis, Sisters of Mercy, Sisters of Our Lady of Mercy, Sisters of Charity, Sisters of Charity of Emmitsburg, Sisters of Charity of Nazareth, and Sisters of Divine Providence (Jacob: 127). The monument is totally without political bias, making no reference to either the Union or the Confederacy, but instead alluding to the universality of the nursing profession. The inscription above the bas-relief plaque reads:

The Ladies' Auxiliary of the Ancient Order of Hibernians erected this monument to commemorate the twelve orders of nuns who cared for sick and wounded soldiers on both sides during the Civil War. *Photo courtesy of Bull Run Civil War Round Table.*

> They comforted the dying, nursed the wounded, carried hope to the imprisoned, gave in His name a drink of water to the thirsty.

Engraved above the inscription is a cross inside a wreath. Inscribed on the base, beneath the bronze bas-relief panel, is:

> To the memory and in honor of the various orders of sisters who gave their services as nurses on battlefields and in hospitals during the Civil War.

Flanking the plaque are bronze sculptures personifying Patriotism and Peace, who are facing north and south, respectively. A set of stone stairs on either side leads up to the panel, allowing visitors a closer look at the detail of the twelve life-sized bas-reliefs.

Connor began working on the memorial in 1919, after incorporating several changes requested by the Commission of Fine Arts. A few years earlier, he had sculpted the statue of Robert Emmet, which at that time was located at the Smithsonian Institution, as well as the statue of Bishop John Carroll, at Georgetown University (ibid: 126-127).

The Ladies' Auxiliary of the Ancient Order of Hibernians paid for the monument, and originally wanted it placed in Arlington National Cemetery, but the War Department refused. Spearheading the creation of the memorial was Ellen Jolly, who was president of the Auxiliary. For his work, Connor received $50,000.

Location: Rhode Island Avenue and M Street, N.W., opposite Saint Matthew's Cathedral.

Philip H. Sheridan

Gutzon Borglum, best known for his work on Mount Rushmore in South Dakota, imbued his eleven-foot bronze sculpture of General Philip Sheridan and his horse, Rienzi, with a vivid sense of power, poise, and alacrity. Sheridan's right arm is extended, his hand waving the hat that he is clutching. His left hand grips the reins. Rienzi is leaning back slightly on his haunches, his front legs splayed wide as if he is screeching to a halt. Borglum's aim was to capture steed and rider following the general's famous ride from Winchester, Virginia, to Cedar Creek, where Sheridan rallied his retreating troops to victory against encroaching Confederate forces led by Jubal Early. This October 19, 1864 event spawned the poem "Sheridan's Ride," by Thomas B. Read. Read's poem, like Borglum's sculpture, glorifies horse as much as rider:

> ... And when their statues are placed on high,
> Under the dome of the Union sky,
> The American soldier's Temple of Fame;
> There with the glorious general's name,
> Be it said, in letters both bold and bright,
> "Here is the steed that saved the day,
> By carrying Sheridan into the fight,
> From Winchester, twenty miles away!

At the November 25, 1908 dedication, President Theodore Roosevelt recounted Sheridan's illustrious military career, and his staunch dedication to the preservation of the Union. Although the general had been dead twenty years, his legacy was still very much alive. Also in attendance were Sheridan's widow and four children, including Philip Henry Sheridan, Jr.

The Sheridan statue is arguably the finest equestrian sculpture in the capital. Borglum received $50,000, which Congress had appropriated. Originally, John Quincy Adams Ward – who had created the statues of George H. Thomas and James A. Garfield – was commissioned to create a memorial for Sheridan, but arguments between him and Sheridan's family nixed that.

After the Battle of Cedar Creek, Rienzi – whose namesake was a town in Mississippi – was renamed "Winchester" by his master. Sheridan was extremely proud of his horse, citing the animal's speed, power, and remarkable discipline. From 1862 until the end of the war, horse and rider rode in some eighty-five battles. Sheridan once remarked of his sublime steed ". . .he was as cool and quiet under fire as one of my soldiers" (Smithsonian). The stuffed Rienzi is on display at the Smithsonian's National Museum of American History.

Nicknamed "Little Phil," Sheridan more than compensated for his diminutive stature with his bravery and exemplary service to his country. Following the Battle of Cedar Creek, he was placed in charge of the Army of the Potomac. Sheridan died in 1888 at the age of fifty-seven, and was interred in Arlington National Cemetery. Both Albany, New York, and Somerset, Ohio, have claimed him as their native son.

Location: Massachusetts Avenue and 23rd Street, N.W., in Sheridan Circle.

Gutzon Borglum's equestrian statue of General Philip Sheridan is perhaps the most dramatic sculpture of its kind in Washington, D.C. *Photos courtesy of Bull Run Civil War Round Table.*

Robert Emmet

For nearly fifty years, the seven-foot, 1,500-pound bronze statue of martyred Irish patriot Robert Emmet occupied the main rotunda of the Smithsonian Institution's National Museum of Natural History, only to be displaced by a huge, stuffed elephant. The institution's directors decided that Emmet deserved more appropriate surroundings, so he was transplanted to a tiny park at Massachusetts Avenue and 24th Street, N.W., where he stands today (*Washington Post*). The Emmet statue was rededicated on April 22, 1966, shortly after its installment at the new location.

The work of sculptor Jerome Conner (see Bishop John Carroll and Nuns of the Battlefield entries) and architect Richard Murphy, the memorial depicts Emmet addressing the British court that sentenced him to death in 1803 for fomenting a rebellion in Dublin against English rule. At his trial, Emmett was apparently unrepentant and defiant, and invoked George Washington and the United States as paragons of freedom and democracy. The inscription on the front of the green granite pedestal reads: "ROBERT EMMET/IRISH PATRIOT/1778-1803." Quotes from Emmett appear on the back. The memorial was erected in 1917 by Irish-Americans to commemorate Ireland's recent independence from England. Those attending the June 28 dedication heard eulogies from California Senator James D. Phelan and President Woodrow Wilson, and singer John McCormack performed three songs, accompanied by pianists. Formally accepting the Emmet statue on behalf of the Smithsonian was the institution's secretary, Charles D. Walcott.

In preparing his sculptural models, Conner studied sketches of the Irish rebel drawn at his trial, and an actor who had portrayed Emmet in a play modeled for him.

Emmet was a leader of the United Irishmen party, and came from a very wealthy Dublin family. Emmet was educated at

Trinity College, and his father was Ireland's state physician. In organizing the ill-fated July 23, 1803 insurrection, Emmet had hoped to capitalize on England's current war with France. The previous year, he had traveled to the continent and met with Napoleon Bonaparte in an effort to obtain the emperor's assistance. Whether that assistance ever would have come will never be known, as Emmet was too impatient to postpone his plans.

His supporters took up arms against the English in Dublin and several other Irish cities, but were outmatched. Dozens of United Irishmen were executed and many more imprisoned in the wake of the failed coup, and Emmet found himself at the end of the hangman's rope two months later (O'Donnell).

Location: Massachusetts Avenue and 24th Street, N.W.

This memorial to Irish patriot Robert Emmet (1778-1803) had two dedications, one in 1917 and the second in 1966. *Photo by Maureen R. Quinn.*

Quotes from Emmet appear on the back of the pedestal. *Photo by Maureen R. Quinn.*

Samuel Francis Dupont Memorial Fountain

The goddess of Fortune is traditionally represented as a woman, ships were often given feminine names, and an old sailor's superstition held that women on board vessels would bring misfortune upon the crew. A variation of this belief was that only virgins were bad luck, as the ship would resent their never having borne the weight of a man. Given all of this, one might expect the eight-foot statues representing the Wind, the Sea, and the Stars to all be distaff depictions. The inclusion of one male figure around the font of the memorial fountain dedicated to Rear Admiral Samuel Francis Dupont was progressive thinking on the part of sculptor Daniel Chester French and architect Henry Bacon.

The Sea is a sultry young woman with flowing hair, the wet robe which clings to her body accenting her smooth, feminine curves. She is holding a ship in the crook of her right arm, and a seagull perches on her left shoulder. Her celestial counterpart, the Stars, holds a globe in one hand. Her expression is carefree, even cavalier, with none of the patent strain evidenced in pictures of Atlas lugging the world atop his shoulders. But the Wind, holding a large sea shell, is a young man. Together they represent the three essential elements of a sailor's journey.

Although part of the inscription around the base of the fountain reads ""ERECTED BY THE CONGRESS OF THE UNITED STATES," it was the wealthy Dupont family that footed the fountain's nearly $80,000 cost in 1921. The fountain occupies a plaza in the center of a busy traffic circle in downtown Washington, D.C. Nearly forty years earlier, Irish sculptor Launt Thompson created a bronze statue of Dupont, which was removed by the Dupont family in 1916, and placed at their estate in Winterthur, Delaware. The public seemed to like French and Bacons's new tribute much better than Thompson's old one.

Allegorical figures representing the Wind, the Sea, and the Stars surround the base of the Samuel Francis Dupont Memorial Fountain. Sculpted by Daniel Chester French and designed by Henry Bacon, the fountain replaced an earlier bronze statue by Launt Thompson. *Photo courtesy of Bull Run Civil War Round Table.*

Dupont was lauded as a hero after his capture of Port Royal, South Carolina, shortly after the start of the Civil War. Had his military successes continued unabated, he might have been named the United States Navy's first full admiral instead of David G. Farragut. Two years later, however, Dupont was relieved of his command of the South Atlantic Blockading Squadron after a humiliating defeat in Charleston Harbor. He was a bitter, broken man at his death in 1865, at the age of sixty-two.

Location: Massachusetts and Connecticut avenues N.W., in Dupont Circle.

Samuel Gompers

Born in London in 1850, Samuel Gompers founded the American Federation of Labor and became the organization's first president in 1886, serving in that capacity until his death in 1924. In the four decades that Gompers was at the helm, the AFL's membership increased from 50,000 to three million (AFL-CIO). In 1955, the group merged with the Congress of Industrial Organizations, forming the AFL-CIO.

As a youth, Gompers had little formal schooling. His first job was rolling cigars with his father at the age of ten. In 1863, the Gompers family moved to New York City, where young Sam continued his line of work, later serving as president of Local 144 of the Cigar Makers International Union (ibid). Throughout his life, Gompers campaigned hard for employee rights, and among his accomplishments were the elimination of child labor and the establishment of the eight-hour workday.

The AFL commissioned Robert Aitken $117,000 to create the memorial to their first and longest-serving president. Aitken is best remembered for his "Equal Justice Under Law" bas-relief, on the pediment above the main entrance to the Supreme Court. The Gompers memorial features a bronze statue of the labor leader, seated on a ledge of a granite stele that is flanked by walls bearing lengthy inscriptions. Atop each wall, slightly behind the statue of Gompers, are allegorical figures relating to the American labor movement. Two burly, bare-chested men stand on either side of the granite stele, shaking hands. On the left wall, slightly behind one of the hand-shakers, are two female figures. One is standing, holding a Roman fasces against her right side. The other is seated, nursing a baby. On the right wall, slightly behind the second hand-shaker, is a female angel, and seated at her feet is a man reading a book.

The dedication for the Gompers memorial was held on October 7, 1933. President Franklin D. Roosevelt, who had been a close friend of Gompers, spoke of their common ideals, hardships, and triumphs. The president then compared the struggles of World War I to those faced by working men and women during the Great Depression, which was then in its fourth year. Roosevelt acknowledged that the labor movement was not without its problems, but said that these were due to human venality, not organized labor per se.

Location: 10th Street and Massachusetts Avenue, N.W.

SAMUEL GOMPERS

"SO LONG AS WE HAVE HELD FAST TO VOLUNTARY PRINCIPLES AND HAVE BEEN ACTUATED AND INSPIRED BY THE SPIRIT OF SERVICE WE HAVE SUSTAINED OUR FORWARD PROGRESS AND WE HAVE MADE OUR LABOR MOVEMENT SOMETHING TO BE RESPECTED AND ACCORDED A PLACE IN THE COUNCILS OF OUR REPUBLIC WHERE WE HAVE BLUNDERED INTO TRYING TO FORCE A POLICY OR A DECISION EVEN THOUGH WISE AND RIGHT WE HAVE IMPEDED IF NOT INTERRUPTED THE REALIZATION OF OUR OWN AIMS."

"NO LASTING GAIN HAS EVER COME FROM COMPULSION. IF WE SEEK TO FORCE WE BUT TEAR APART THAT WHICH UNITED IS INVINCIBLE. THERE IS NO WAY WHEREBY OUR LABOR MOVEMENT MAY BE ASSURED SUSTAINED PROGRESS IN DETERMINING ITS POLICIES AND ITS PLANS OTHER THAN SINCERE DEMOCRATIC DELIBERATION UNTIL A UNANIMOUS DECISION IS REACHED. THIS MAY SEEM A CUMBROUS SLOW METHOD TO THE IMPATIENT BUT THE IMPATIENT ARE MORE CONCERNED FOR IMMEDIATE RESULTS THAN FOR THE EDUCATION OF CONSTRUCTIVE DEVELOPMENT."

The elaborate monument to Samuel Gompers, founder of the American Federation of Labor. Sculptor Robert Aitken received $117,000 for the work. *Photos by Maureen R. Quinn.*

Samuel Hahnemann

Washington, D.C. has a number of private monuments, those that immortalize men and women whose actions and contributions, significant though they may have been, are limited in scope to specific organizations or institutions. Even if their contributions were such that they extended the limited boundaries of their particular fields, these individuals' names are unfamiliar to the general public. Maybe the builders of these monuments to obscure heroes hoped to ignite in the ignorant passerby a spark of interest, which would eventually lead to further inquiries.

Homeopathy is a branch of medicine that prescribes drugs which induce symptoms of the person's particular ailment in order to cure him, similar to the "hair from the dog that bit you" theory. One example is when a doctor injects a patient with allergens – substances that cause allergic reactions – so that the patient can eventually build up a tolerance (AIH). Homeopathy was founded in 1800 by C.F. (Christian Friedrich) Samuel Hahnemann, a German physician. In 1844, the year after Hahnemann died, the American Institute of Homeopathy was founded.

In 1900, the AIH erected a memorial to Hahnemann in Washington, D.C.'s Scott Circle. Fundraising efforts had begun earnestly eight years earlier. A five-man panel that included Daniel Chester French selected Charles Henry Niehaus's design from about thirty submitted. Niehaus, the son of German immigrants, was well-known for his portrait sculptures. His art concentrated more on raw emotion and energy rather than on minute detail. Assisting him in the design of the memorial was New York architect Julius F. Harder. The cost of the project was $75,000.

A robed, bronze figure of Hahnemann sits contemplatively in an alcove framed by Ionic columns. The doctor's head rests on his right hand, his elbow propped up on the arm rest. Above him is a mosaic made of colored glass tiles. On either side of the curved granite wall behind him are two bronze panels, each depicting different periods in Hahnemann's life. Below the panels are benches, and four steps in the front lead up to the plaza.

The inscription below Hahnemann reads *Similia Similibus Curentur*, Latin for "Likes are cured by likes." Another Latin inscription reads *In Omnibus Caritas* – "In all things charity" – and another in German which reads *Die Milde Macht ist Gross* – "Gentle Power is great" (Rosales and Jobe). Inscribed on the portico above the alcove is "HAHNEMANN."

On June 21, 2000, 100 years after the initial unveiling, the Hahnemann Memorial was rededicated by the AIH. Four years later, the AIH did a $30,000 restoration of the memorial, which included steam cleaning the granite surfaces, replacing some of the square glass mosaic tiles, and planting an Oak tree where one had stood at the time of the original dedication.

Location: Massachusetts Avenue and 16th Street, in Scott Circle.

The Samuel Hahnemann Monument, surrounded by fall foliage. *Photos courtesy of Sandra M. Chase, MD, DHt.*

Taras Shevchenko

The move to establish a memorial for the nineteenth-century Ukrainian poet Taras Shevchenko (1814-1861) was met with vehement objection by residents and non-residents of Washington, D.C. alike. Shevchenko, who was jailed because of his anti-Czarist sentiments and died in prison, was revered in the former Soviet Union as an inspiration to the communist cause. But a line from one of Shevchenko's poems praises George Washington, which was probably what prompted a group of Ukrainian nationals to have the statue erected in 1964 (Goode: 298).

The memorial features a fourteen-foot bronze statue, sculpted by Leo Mol. The statue stands next to a shorter, rectangular slab of granite with a bas-relief of the Greek god Prometheus. According to mythology, Prometheus stole fire to give to mankind. For this he was punished by Zeus by being chained to a rock while a vulture tore out and ate his liver, which continually regenerated so that Prometheus was forced to endure daily torment. According to legend, he was eventually rescued by Hercules. The placement of Prometheus alongside Shevchenko is an allusion to the martyrdom that the historical and mythological figures share with each other. The memorial also features markers with Shevchenko's poetry.

A three-hour parade preceded the June 27, 1964 unveiling, as hundreds of marchers lined up at the Ellipse south of the White house, then proceeded north on 15th Street, west on New York Avenue to Pennsylvania Avenue, and finally north to a triangular plot of ground at 22nd, 23rd, and P streets, where the memorial stands (*Washington Post*). The statue was unveiled by former President Dwight D. Eisenhower.

Location: P and 22nd streets.

Thomas Hopkins Gallaudet

This memorial, on the grounds of the Gallaudet University for the Deaf, was created by Daniel Chester French in 1888. The statue depicts educator Reverend Thomas Hopkins Gallaudet helping young Alice Cogswell form the letter "A" in sign language. Gallaudet is seated in a chair, while little Alice stands beside him.

Alice's father, Mason, was a neighbor of Gallaudet's. Later, the two of them co-founded the American School for the Deaf, in Hartford, Connecticut, along with French educator Laurent Clerc. Gallaudet's son, Edward, became the first president of Gallaudet University in 1857, which at that time was called the Columbian Institution for the Instruction of the Deaf, Dumb, and Blind, a name which would fall quite short of meeting today's standards of political sensitivity.

The thirty-eight-year-old sculptor took his commission very seriously, apparently giving it more importance than his personal life. When Augustus Saint-Gaudens saw the model for the Gallaudet memorial and remarked that the legs looked too short, French postponed his own wedding for a month while he made the necessary corrections (Cra-ven: 397). The memorial was dedicated in 1889.

Location: Florida Avenue, between 6th Street and West Virginia Avenue, Gallaudet University campus.

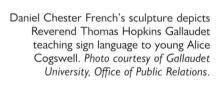

Daniel Chester French's sculpture depicts Reverend Thomas Hopkins Gallaudet teaching sign language to young Alice Cogswell. *Photo courtesy of Gallaudet University, Office of Public Relations.*

Titanic Memorial

In the early morning hours of April 15, 1912, the RMS *Titanic* sunk to an icy death 13,000 feet below the cold waters of the North Atlantic, less than three hours after a huge iceberg punctured her starboard hull. A mere five days earlier, she had embarked on her maiden voyage from Southampton, England, amidst great fanfare. Two-thirds of the people on board perished, many of whom were immigrants headed for a new life in America. In stark contrast were millionaires and their wives, business magnates and dignitaries, and those with just slightly less luxurious accommodations in second class. Built between 1909 and 1911 for the White Star Line, the ship had been compared to a floating palace, complete with state rooms, parlors, squash courts, a gymnasium, gilded chandeliers, elevators, and intricately-carved balustrades flanking the grand staircase leading from the D deck to the first class promenade deck. From stern to bow, the *Titanic* stretched 882 feet, was ninety-two feet wide, and weighed over 40,000 tons unladen. Four massive smoke stacks protruded from the main deck, in between the fore and rear masts. The *Titanic* truly lived up to her name.

Although designer A.M. Carlisle intended the ship to be as sturdy as she was stately, he apparently overlooked several possible safety issues. The hull contained fifteen bulkheads, individual compartments to contain water in the event of a rupture. The walls separating the bulkheads were only ten feet high, however, not high enough to completely seal each bulkhead. Once the hull began taking on water, all of the bulkheads were eventually flooded (Adams:13).

Congressional approval for a memorial to the *Titanic's* victims came in 1917, a year following the erection of a memorial in Southampton, England. Gertrude Vanderbilt Whitney won a national competition open to female sculptors. Her granite memorial features an eighteen-foot man standing atop a six-foot pedestal, with his arms outstretched. The memorial sits on a thirty-foot long, rectangular plaza surrounded by low walls on the rear and sides, and was designed by architect Henry Bacon.

The personification of self-sacrifice, the statue represents the men who relinquished their life preservers and spaces on life rafts to ensure that the women and children escaped first. As a result, the majority of the 1,500 people who perished in the disaster were men, a fact cited by Massachusetts Representative Robert Luce at the memorial's May 26, 1931 dedication. The sculptor had a personal connection to maritime tragedies, having lost her brother in 1915 when a German submarine torpedoed the *Lusitania*. The sinking of this ship was one of the events that helped sway a reluctant America to enter the Great War two years later.

Among those attending the dedication were President Herbert Hoover and his wife, and members of the memorial association that spearheaded the fundraising. The eleven-member executive committee included former First Lady Helen Herron Taft.

The piece was officially known as the Women's *Titanic* Memorial, because the all-female committee members wanted to honor the men who put the safety of the women and children first, often consigning themselves to watery graves. This ostensible act of chivalry, however, was ordered by Captain Edward Smith and his crew. Nonetheless, the inscription reads:

> To the brave men who perished in the wreck of the *Titanic*, April 15, 1912. They gave their lives that women and children might be saved."

One of the casualties of the *Titanic* was Francis D. Millet, vice-chairman of the Commission of Fine Arts, the organization that has overseen landscaping, architecture, and design of the capital since 1910.

Location: P and 4th streets.

Winfield Scott

Sculpted by Henry Kirke Brown, this bronze equestrian statue of Lieutenant General Winfield Scott is widely regarded as awkward, if not comical. A dispute over whether Scott should be riding upon a mare or a stallion led to a compromise which produced a mount whose head and tail are disproportionately large for its body. The figure of Scott – his right hand arrogantly resting on his hip – makes the general appear like a fat old man, one that the skimpy horse on which he is riding would strain to support (Jacob: 100-101). The name "SCOTT" is inscribed on the front of the statue's granite pedestal. Horse and rider are cast in bronze, from melted-down cannons seized during the Mexican War. The statue was erected without ceremony in 1874, eight years after Scott's death.

Known as "Old Fuss 'n' Feathers" because of his meticulous nature, Scott had his heyday during the Mexican War, but his military career spanned nearly sixty years. By the beginning of the Civil War, he was obese and in declining health. He died in 1866, at the age of seventy-nine. Scott was instrumental in founding the Soldiers' Home at 3700 North Capitol Street circa 1850, and about twenty years later, a bronze statue of him was erected there. An admirer of fellow Virginian Robert E. Lee, Scott thought that Lee would be an excellent choice to command the Union army. However, Lee turned down President Lincoln's request to do this, choosing to fight for his native Virginia instead. As much as Lee was calumniated in the North for choosing the Confederacy, Scott was as maligned in the South, particularly in Virginia, when he supported the Union cause. Scott ran for the presidency on the Whig Party ticket in 1852, losing to Franklin Pierce.

Location: Massachusetts Avenue and 16th Street N.W., in Scott Circle.

This equestrian statue of General Winfield Scott is not one of Henry Kirke Brown's best works.
Photo courtesy of Bull Run Civil War Round Table.

Bibliography

Adams, Simon. *Titanic*. New York: DK Publishing, 2004.

AFL-CIO. 2005. 8 July 2005 <http://www.aflcio.org>.

African American Civil War Memorial. African American Civil War Memorial Freedom Foundation. 24 Dec. 2004 <http://www.afroamcivilwar.org>.

"Albert Gallatin." *United States Department of the Treasury* 15 Mar. 2005 <http://www.treas.gov/education/history/secretaries/agallatin.shtml>.

"Alexander Pushkin." *Webster's NewWorld™ Encylopedia*. 1992.

American Battle Monuments Commission (ABMC) Operations. "RE: Research for a book." E-mail to the author. 14 Jan. 2005.

American Institute of Homeopathy. 6 Apr. 2005 <http://www.homeopathyusa.org>.

American Red Cross. "Armenia Thanks America In Ceremony At American Red Cross." Press release. Sept. 1990.

American Red Cross. *DEDICATION OF THE MEMORIAL TO JANE A. DELANO AND THE 296 Nurses Who Died in the War, 1914-1918*. 1934.

The American Red Cross National News Service. "General Clark Pays Tribute To ARC Dead At Ceremony." Press release. 25 June 1959.

Ancient & Accepted Scottish Rite of Free-Masonry. *Transactions of the Supreme Council, 33°, for the Southern Jurisdiction of the United States of America, sitting at the City of Washington, in October, 1899*. 301-304.

_____. *Transactions of the Supreme Council, 33°, for the Southern Jurisdiction of the United States of America*. 1901. 51-55, 82, 135-140.

Anderson, Jewel. Telephone interview. 27 June 2005.

"Andrew Mellon Fountain Here Is Dedicated." *Washington Post* 10 May 1952.

Arlington National Cemetery. 29 May 2005 <http://www.arlingtoncemetery.org>.

Armstrong, Tom et al, eds. *200 Years of American Sculpture*. New York: Whitney Museum of American Art, 1976. 120.

"At Ceremonies Honoring Uruguayan Patriot." *New York Times* 20 June 1950: 13.

"Baron von Steuben." *Historic Valley Forge* 2005 Independence Hall Association. 5 July 2005 <http://www.ushistory.org/valleyforge/served/steuben. html>.

Barringer, Felicity. "Thousands Feared Dead in Soviet Caucasus Quake." *New York Times* 8 Dec. 1988: A1+.

Bartholomew, Ann E. "RE: Red Cross Square Statuary." E-mail to the author. 14 June 2005.

Baym, Nina et al, eds. *The Norton Anthology of American Literature*. 1979. 2nd ed. 2 vols. New York: W.W. Norton & Co., 1985. 1277-1278.

Berry, Nancy. "New GW Statue Honors Russian Cultural Icon." *By George!* 3 Oct. 2000, 1+.

Blackstone, William. *Commentaries on the Laws of England*. Oxford, England: Clarendon Press: 1765-1769. *Blackstone's Commentaries on the Laws of England*. 2003. The Avalon Project at Yale Law School. 6 July 2005 <http://www.yale.edu/lawweb/avalon/blackstone/blacksto.htm>.

Bolotin, Norman. *Civil War A to Z*. New York: Dutton Children's Book, 2002. 37, 42-43, 83-84.

Boltuck, Richard. Photograph of the sculpture "Grief" in Rock Creek Cemetery. *PBASE.com* 23 March 2003. 23 December 2004 <http://www.pbase.com/rboltuck/image/14824846>.

Bowen-Haskell, E. Gordon et al. *Sea Raiders of the American Revolution: The Continental Navy in European Waters*. Washington, D.C.: Naval Historical Center, 2003. 47. *Naval Historical Center*. 10 Nov. 2003. United States Navy. 15 May, 2005 <http://www.history.navy.mil/bios/jones_jp_did.htm>.

"Boy Scout Memorial." *National Park Service U.S. Department of the Interior*. 26 Apr. 2003. 1 Mar. 2005 <http://www.nps.gov/whho/PPSth/boysctmem/>.

Calloway, Heather K. "RE: Research for a book." E-mail to the author. 22 Feb. 2005.

"Captain John Barry." *Naval Historical Center* 27 Aug. 2002 Department of the Navy, 17 May, 2005 < http://www.history.navy.mil/bios/barry_john.htm>.

Cary, Francis. "Life of Dante." *The Divine Comedy*. By Dante Alighieri. Trans. Francis Cary. Seacaucus, NJ: Chartwell Books, 1982. 5-8.

"Casualties: U.S. Navy and Marine Corps Personnel Killed and Wounded in Wars, Conflicts, Terrorist Acts, and Other Hostile Incidents." 14 Dec. 2004 *Department of the Navy*. 1 Apr. 2005 <http://www.history. navy.mil/faqs/faq56-1.htm>.

"Chickamauga." *CWSAC Battle Summaries*. American Battlefield Protection Program, National Park Service. 21 Apr. 2005 <http://www.cr.nps.gov/hps/abpp/index.htm>.

"Chief Justice John Marshall." *U.S. District Court. District of Columbia*. 22 Mar. 2005 <http://www.dcd. uscourts.gov/marshall.html>.

The Civil War. Prod. Ken Burns. 1989. DVD. PBS DVD Gold, 1990.

"Clark Mills again. The Egyptian obelisk of Murder Bay." Letter to the editor. *Washington Post* Archives. 19 Dec. 1877. 22 Oct. 2004 <http://www.washington post.com>.

Clopton, Willard. "Rough Rider 'Rides' Again." *Washington Post* 28 Oct. 1967: A1+.

"Commodore John Barry, USN, (1745-1803)." *Naval Historical Center* 17 Sept. 2002 Department of the Navy. 17 May, 2005 <http://www.history.navy.mil/photos/pers-us/uspers-b/j-barry.htm>.

"The Compromise of 1850 and the Fugitive Slave Act." *PBS Online* PBS 11 May, 2005 <http://www.pbs.org/wgbh/aia/part4/4p2951.html>.

Craven, Wayne. *Sculpture in America*. New York: Thomas E. Crowell, 1968. 87-88, 160, 168, 170, 172, 227-228, 237, 240, 251, 394-395, 397, 426-427, 453-454, 477, 698, 708.

"Cuba's Gift Vase Arrives in City." *Washington Post* 5 Dec. 1928.

The Declaration of Independence. Ed. Thomas Kindig. 19 July 2005 <http://www.ushistory.org/declaration>.

"The Delano Memorial Unveiled." *The American Journal of Nursing*, June 1934: 523-526.

De Vries, Charles. "Luther in Stone and Bronze." *The Lutheran Standard* 5 Nov. 1963: 14-17.

Doss, Karen. "John Carroll Restoration Underway." *Blue & Gray* 23 Sept. 1990: 8.

"Edmund Burke (1729-1797)." *Historic Figures* BBC. 24 May 2005 <http://www.bbc.co.uk/history/historic _figures/burke_edmund>.

"The Education of Henry Adams." *C-SPAN American Writers II*. 2004. 15 Oct. 2004 <http://www.american writers.org/classroom/videolesson/clips19_adams. asp>.

The Einstein Memorial at the National Academies. A Visitor's Guide. (Washington, D.C.: National Academies, n.d.)

"Epigrams from Gandhi." *Mahatma Gandhi*. 3 Mar. 2005. Bombay Sarvodaya Mandal and Sarvodaya Ashram, Nagpur. 23 Mar. 2005 <http://www.mkgandhi.org/epigrams/c.htm#top>.

Evans, Diane Carlson. "Moving a Vision: The Vietnam Women's Memorial." *Vietnam Women's Memorial Foundation* 24 Nov. 2004 <http://www.vietnam womensmemorial.org>.

"Fasces." *Webster's New World Dictionary*. Third College Edition. 1988.

Fernandez-Duque, Silvina. "First Division Monument." *National Park Service U.S. Department of the Interior*. 23 Apr. 2003. 1 Mar. 2005 <http://www.nps.gov/whho/PPSth/1stdivmon/index.htm>.

Field, Cynthia R. "The Adams Memorial." *Smithsonian Preservation Quarterly*. Summer/Fall 1995 Edition. (1995). 23 Dec. 2004 <http://www.si.edu/oahp/spq/spq95sf1.htm>.

Find A Grave. 12 Oct. 2004. <http://www.findagrave. com>.

Flemming, Sheila Y. "The Life of Dr. Mary McLeod Bethune." Bethune-Cookman College. 23 May 2005 <http://www.cookman.edu>.

Forgey, Benjamin. "Bronze Tribute to an Iron Will; Virginia Statesman George Mason Takes His Seat on the Mall." *Washinton Post* 9 Apr. 2002: C1.

"Frederick Douglass." *The New Encylopaedia Britannica*. 2002.

Freidel, Frank and Hugh S. Sidey. *The Presidents of the United States of America*. Washington, D.C.: White House Historical Association, n.d. *The White House*. 21 Oct. 2004 <http://www.whitehouse.gov/history/presidents>.

Fritz, Jean. *The Great Little Madison*. New York: G.P. Putnam's Sons, 1989.

Gallaudet University. Lincoln Circle Walking Tour. Washington, D.C.: Gallaudet University, n.d.

"Gen. Greene's Bones Found." *Washington Post* 5 Mar. 1901: 8.

"Gen. Greene's Interment." *Washington Post* 11 Apr.1902: 1.

The George Mason National Memorial. 10 July 2005 <http://gunstonhall.org/memorialgarden/>.

Getlein, Frank. "Monuments and Memorials." *Washington, D.C.: A Smithsonian Book Of The Nation's Capital*. Ed. Patricia Gallagher. Washington, D.C.: Smithsonian Institution, 1992. 120-140.

"Gift." *Washington Post* 15 Apr. 1966: B2.

Glory. Dir. Edward Zwick. Perf. Matthew Broderick, Denzel Washington, Morgan Freeman. 1989. DVD. Columbia Tristar Home Video, n.d.

Goode, James M. *The Outdoor Sculpture of Washington, D.C.* Washington, D.C.: Smithsonian Institution Press, 1974.

Gooder, Jean. Introduction. *The Education of Henry Adams*. 1918. By Henry Adams. Ed. Jean Gooder. London: Penguin Books, 1995. vii-xliii.

Gugarats, Haik. "RE: Research for a book." E-mail to the author. 22 Feb. 2005.

"Guilford Courthouse." *National Park Service*. 23 June 23 2005 <http://www.nps.gov/guco/>.

Hale, Edward Everett. "Captain Nathan Hale (1755-1776)." 2002. The Connecticut Society of the Sons of the American Revolution, Inc. 6 June 2005 <http://www.ctssar.org/patriots/nathan_hale.htm>.

Hathaway, Hanson H. "Work of Bartlett Reaches Capital from Temple in London." *Washington Post* 12 Aug. 1943: B1.

Hearn, Chester G. *Admiral David Glasgow Farragut: The Civil War Years*. Annapolis: Naval Institute Press, 1998.

"Hendricks, Thomas Andrews, (1819-1885)." *Biographical Directory of the United States Congress*. 1 Apr. 1, 2005 <http://bioguide.congress.gov/scripts/biodisplay.pl?index=H000493>.

The Holy Bible. New York: B and S Publishing House, 1947. 55.

"Homeopathy." *Webster's New World Dictionary*. Third College Edition. 1988.

"Honor Irish Patriot." *Washington Post* 29 June 1917: 7.

"Honor Steuben Today." *Washington Post* 7 Dec. 1910: 1+.

"Hoover Dedicates Buchanan Statue." *New York Times* 27 June 1930.

Hunter, Charlayne. "20,000 at Unveiling of Statue to Mary Bethune in Capital." *New York Times* 11 July 1974.

"Irish Rebel's Statue to be Unveiled." *Washington Post* 12 Apr. 1966: A11.

Iwo Jima. 2004. 27 Apr. 2005 <http://www.iwojima. com>.

Jackson, S. "Early History of Photography." Montana State University. 19 May 2005 <http://gemini.msu. montana.edu/~photohst/mta303/>.

Jacob, Kathryn Allamong. *Testament to Union: Civil War Monuments in Washington, D.C.* Baltimore: Johns Hopkins University Press, 1998.

"The Jane A. Delano Memorial in Washington." *The Red Cross Courier* July 1933: 7.

Jerome Connor [sic]. Georgetown University Archives, Washington, D.C., n.d.

Joan of Arc. Dir. Victor Fleming. Perf. Ingrid Bergman, José Ferrer. 1948. DVD. Image Entertainment, 2004.

"JOHN CARROL STATUE REVISITED." *Blue & Gray* 23 Sept. 1990: 8.

"John Marshall." *The Supreme Court Historical Society*. 22 Mar. 2005 <http://www.supremecourthistory.org/02_history/subs_timeline/images_chiefs/004.html>.

John Paul Jones: Commemoration at Annapolis, April 24, 1906. Washington, D.C.: Government Printing Office, 1907. 165-184. *Naval Historical Center.* 10 Nov. 2003. Department of the Navy. 15 May, 2005 <http://www.history.navy.mil/bios/jones_jp_ chron.htm>.

The John Salling Page. Ed. Peter O'Malley. 11 Feb. 2005. <http://www.omalco.com/salling.htm>.

Johnston, Joyce. *Washington, D.C.* Minneapolis: Lerner Publications Company, 2003. 8.

"Joseph Henry." *Washington Post* 20 Apr. 1883: 2.

"The Joseph Henry Statue." *Washington Post* 4 Apr. 1883: 4.

Joyce, John A. "As He Led in Battle." *Washington Post* 13 May 1896: 1+.

Keller, Mollie. *Alexander Hamilton.* Consulting Ed. Richard B. Morris. New York: Franklin Watts, 1986.

Kent, Deborah. *America the Beautiful: Washington, D.C.* Chicago: Children's Press, 1991.

Knapp, Roberta and Bob Magee. *Ride With Me: The Washington, D.C. Story.* CD-ROM. Bethesda: RWM Associates, 2002.

Knight, Glenn B. "Brief History of the Grand Army of the Republic." *Sons of Union Veterans of the Civil War.* 18 Dec. 2004 <http://suvcw.org/gar.htm>.

Kohler, Sue A. *The Commission of Fine Arts: A Brief History, 1910-1995.* Washington, D.C.: The Commission of Fine Arts, 1995.

Kreis, Steven. "Edmund Burke, 1729-1797." *Lectures on Modern European Intellectual History.* 13 May 2004. The History Guide. 24 May 2005 <http://www. historyguide.org/intellect/burke>.

Krinsley, Daniel B. "An Unexpected Rendezvous at the Cosmos Club on Lafayette Square." *Cosmos Journal.* 1998. 23 Dec. 2004 <http://www.cosmos-club.org/journals/1998/krinsley.html>.

"LAFAYETTE PARK HISTORIC DISTRICT." National Park Service. 26 Apr. 2005 <http://www.cr.nps.gov/nr/travel/wash/dc30.htm>.

Lawson, Don. *The United States in World War I. The Story of General John J. Pershing and the American Expeditionary Forces.* New York: Abelard-Schuman, 1963. 15, 22-24, 59-61, 148.

Leisenring, L.M. Outline History of the Statue of Martin Luther, Washington, D.C. 29 Feb. 1956.

Lewis, Jone Johnson. "Isabella I of Spain." *About.com.* 12 July 2005 <http://womenshistory.about.com/cs/medrenqueens/p/p_isabella_i.htm>.

Liberty! The American Revolution. Dir. Ellen Hovde and Muffie Meyer. 1997. DVD, 3 vol. PBS, 2004.

Line, William. "Boy Scout Memorial." E-mail to the author. 21 Mar. 2005.

Llewellyn, Robert. *Washington, the Capital.* 1981. Charlottesville, VA: Thomasson-Grant, 1984.

"Mahatma Gandhi Memorial." *Embassy of India.* 23 Mar. 2005 <http://www.indianembassy.org/gandhi/index.html>.

"Marine Corps Marathon 2004. Race Route Guide." *Marine Corps Marathon.* 2004. Marine Corps Marathon. 14 July 2005 <www.marinemarathon.com/forms/RouteGuide.doc>.

"The Marshall Court.1801-1835." *The Supreme Court Historical Society.* 22 Mar. 2005 <http://www.supremecourthistory.org/02_history/subs_history/02_c04.html>.

McCardle, Dorothy. "45-ton Rock for LBJ Memorial Grove." *Washington Post* 14 Aug. 1975: C2.

McNair, Marie. "Uruguay's Embassy Celebrates Unveiling of Hero's Statue." *Washington Post* 20 June 1950, B3.

"Medal of Honor Recipients: World War I." 1 Sept. 2004. *The United States Army.* 2 Mar. 2005 <http://www.army.mil/cmh-pg/mohwwi.htm>.

"Memorial Approved for Early Settlers." *Washington Post* 15 Feb. 1936: 5.

Mendelsohn, Bruce R. "NLEOM Information for your Book." E-mail to the author. 3 Feb. 2005.

A Mighty Fortress is Our God. Martin Luther. 10 Mar. 2003. KDG Wittenburg. 2 June 2005 <http://www. luther.de/en>.

Miller, Nathan. *The U.S. Navy. An Illustrated History.* American Heritage Publishing Co., 1977. 204, 209, 227.

Murdock, Myrtle Cheney. *Your Memorials in Washington.* Washington, D.C.: Monumental Press, 1952. 25-30, 72-74.

"NAS Building – The Einstein Memorial." *National Academy of Sciences.* 2005. 21 Feb. 2005 <http://www4.nas.edu/nas/nashome.nsf?OpenDatabase>.

National Academy of Sciences. *The Albert Einstein Centennial Convocation.* 1979.

_____. "ACADEMY DEDICATES MEMORIAL TO ALBERT EINSTEIN." *News from the National Academy of Sciences.* 1979.

National Law Enforcement Officers Memorial Fund. 24 Jan. 2005 <http://www.nleomf.com>.

National Society Daughters of the American Revolution. *A Century of Service: the story of The DAR.* Washington, D.C.: National Society Daughters of the American Revolution, 1991. 26-27.

National WWII Memorial. 2003. 29 Nov. 2004 <http://www.wwiimemorial.com>.

Noyes, Clara D. "Unveiling of Memorial to Our Heroic Nurses." *The Red Cross Courier,* June 1934: 358-359.

O'Donnell, Ruán. "Robert Emmet: enigmatic revolutionary." *Irish Democrat.* 18 July 2003. Connolly Publications, Ltd. Ed. David Granville. 24 June 2005 <http://www.irishdemocrat.co.uk/features/emmet-enigma/>.

Office of the Curator, Supreme Court of the United States. *Contemplation of Justice and Authority of Law Information Sheet.*

"On Pedestal Of Fame." *Washington Post* 19 Jan. 1900.

On Red Cross Square. Washington, D.C.: American Red Cross, 1979.

"Parks and Recreation." *National Park Service. U.S. Department of the Interior.* 9 Nov. 2004 <http://data2.itc.nps.gov/parksearch/atoz.cfm>.

"Photographers Here Honor Louis Daguerre." *Washington Post* 8 Jan. 1939, 2.

"President Enthusiastic In His Speech Praising The Deeds Of John Barry Dedicating Naval Statue In Memory." *Washington Post* 17 May 1914.

Public Relations Service, Boy Scouts of America. "COMMEMO-RATIVE TRIBUTE TO SCOUTING UNVEILED." Press release. 1964.

Quinn, Maureen R. "Compiled data, Mall Monuments." E-mail to the author. 7 Jan. 2005.

Rambow, John D., Ed. *Fodor's 04 Washington, D.C.* New York: Fodor's Travel Publications, 2004.

Read, Thomas Buchanan. "Sheridan's Ride." *Bartleby.com.* 22 Apr. 2005 <http://www.bartleby.com/102/150.html>.

Reps, John W. *Washington on view: the nation's capital since 1790.* Chapel Hill: University of North Carolina Press, 1991. 8, 87, 203, 216, 240, 242, 244, 246, 258, 266.

The Republic of Virtue. Narr. Robert Hughes. Videocassette. PBS Home Video®. 1996.

"Rienzi or Winchester." *CivilWar@Smithsonian* Smithsonian. 23 Apr. 23 2005 <http://www. civilwar.si.edu/cavalry_winchester.html>.

Roettger, Olinda M. Notes on Luther statues in the United States. 1 Dec. 1955.

"Roosevelt Address on Gompers." *New York Times* 8 Oct. 1933: 3.

Salem, Richard. "Cornerstone Ceremony Held at Taft Memorial." *Washington Post* 14 Apr. 1959: A2.

_____. "Taft Sons Aided Artist Mould Ohioan's Image." *Washington Post* 15 Apr. 1959: A2.

The Seven Wonders of the Ancient World. Ed. Alaa K. Ashmawy. 21 Jan. 2004. 18 Oct. 2004 <http://ce.eng.usf.edu/pharos/wonders>.

"Seven Years' War." *Webster's New World Encyclopedia.* 1992.

"Signer is Honored." *Washington Post* 21 May 1909: 1.

Smith, J.Y. "A Budding Grove." *Washington Post* 7 Apr. 1976: A1+.

"Speaks in Bronze." *Washington Post,* 8 May 1909.

"Stained Glass at Washington National Cathedral. Lecture with Rowan LeCompte, Mar. 24, 2001. *Washington National Cathedral.* 19 Jan. 2005 <http://www.cathedral.org/cathedral/programs/lecompte. html>.

"Statue of Bishop Carroll at Georgetown University." *New York Times* 23 Mar. 1912.

"A Statue of Franklin." *Washington Post* 18 Jan.1889.

"The Statue of Martin Luther." *New York Times* 10 Apr.1884: 5.

"Statues, Monuments and Memorials in National Capital Parks." *National Capital Parks. A History.* 31 July 2003 National Park Service. 3 May, 2005 <http://www.cr.nps.gov/history/online_books/nace/adhia4. htm>.

Stein, Conrad R. *Washington, D.C.* Children's Press, 1999. 126-127.

Stimson, Julia C. "History of the Delano Memorial." *The American Journal of Nursing,* July 1933: 671-674.

Taft, Lorado. *The History of American Sculpture.* London: MacMillan & Co., 1903. 5, 77, 81, 72-88, 121, 123, 142, 212, 218, 222, 227-228, 234-235, 312, 394, 421.

"Thaddeus (Tadeusz) Kosciuszko." *PolskiInternet.com* Cadd Services of Chicago. 12 June 2005 < http://www.polskiinternet.com/english/index.html>.

Tomkins, Sally Kress. *A Quest for Grandeur: Charles Moore and the Federal Triangle*. Washington, D.C.: Smithsonian Institution Press, 1993. 17.

Toto, Christian. "Statue to Honor Russian Poet Set to Debut at GW." By George [George Washington University]! 21 Sept. 1999, 1+.

"Tribute Of Nation." *Washington Post* 25 May 1902, 1+.

"Tributes to Poles." *Washington Post* 12 May 1910, 1+.

Unsolved History: Death of the USS Maine. Dir. Dan Levitt. 2002. DVD. Discovery Channel™, 2004.

"Unveil a Memorial to Second Division." *New York Times* 19 July 1936: N8.

"Unveil Memorial to *Titanic's* Heroes." *New York Times* 27 May 1931: 28.

"Unveiling Rites Set Today For Statue of Shevchenko." *Washington Post* 27 Jun. 1964: C2.

"V.F.W. Gift To Nation Unveiled." *V.F.W. Magazine* Sept. 1976.

"V.F.W. Monument Planned." *V.F.W. Magazine* Sept. 1975.

"V.F.W. 'Torch of Freedom' Symbolic." *V.F.W. Magazine* May 1976.

Vietnam Veterans Memorial Fund. 2003. 26 Oct. 2004 <http://www.vvmf.org>.

"Combat Area Casualties Current File, 6/8/1956 – 1/21/1998." *National Archives and Records Administration*. 27 Oct. 2004 <http://www.archives.gov>.

Wadsworth, Ginger. *Benjamin Banneker, Pioneering Scientist*. Minneapolis: Carolrhoda Books, 2003.

Waldman, Jean. "RE: Jane Delano Memorial (research for a book)." E-mail to the author. 15 Mar. 2005.

Washington, D.C. Convention and Tourism Corporation. 29 Sept. 2004. <http://www.washington.org>.

"The Washington Family." *Sulgrave Manor*. 30 Apr. 2005 <http://www.sulgravemanor.org.uk>.

Wepman, Dennis. *Benito Juarez*. New York: Chelsea House Publishers, 1986.

"Who is that man, anyway?" *KittyTours*. Ed. Jean K. Rosales and Michael R. Jobe. 2 Jan. 2005 <http://www. kittytours.org/thatman2/index.html>.

Willgoren, Debbi. "Founder Finds a Place of Honor; Dignitaries Pay Tribute to George Mason at Dedication of Memorial." *Washinton Post* 10 Apr. 2002: B1.

Zenian, David. "Rebels with a Cause: The Art of Survival without Joining the Communist Party." *Armenian General Benevolent Union* 14 June 2005. AGBU. 14 June 2005 <http://www.agbu.org/agbunews/display. asp?A_ID=80>.

Index

A

Adams Memorial, 163-164
African American Civil War Memorial, 165-167
Alighieri, Dante, 171-172
American Expeditionary Forces Memorial, 80, 98
Armenian Earthquake Memorial, 92-93
Artigas, José, 99
Authority of Law and Contemplation of Justice, 11-13, 43, 147

B

Banneker, Benjamin, Fountain, 34
Barry, John, 79-80
Bethune, Mary McLeod, 89, 196-197
Blackstone, William, 57
Bolivar, Simon, 106, 109-110
Boy Scout Memorial, 68-69
Buchanan, James, 178-181
Burke, Edmund, 172-173

C

Carroll, John, 184-186, 199, 201
Columbus, Christopher, Memorial Fountain, 13-15
Cuban American Friendship Urn, 129

D

Daguerre, Louis, 48
Dante Alighieri, 171-172
Delano, Jane A., Memorial, 96-98
Downing, Andrew Jackson, Memorial Urn, 33
Dupont, Samuel Francis, Memorial Fountain, 72, 203

E

Einstein, Albert, 89-90
Emancipation Monument, 173-175, 178
Emmet, Robert, 199, 201-202
Ericsson, John, 147-148
Eternal Flame, The, 148, 150

F

Farragut, David G., 21, 54, 69-70, 204
First Division Monument, 71-72
Founders of the DAR Memorial, 94-96
Franklin, Benjamin, 35-37, 73, 108, 186
Freedom, Winged Statue, Capitol Dome, 27-29
Future and The Past, The, 38-39

G

Gallatin, Albert, 62-63
Gallaudet, Thomas Hopkins, 72, 119, 209-210
Gandhi, Mahatma, 191-193
Garfield, James A., 16-17, 59, 118, 200
Gompers, Samuel, 204-206
Grand Army of the Republic Monument, 41-43
Grant, Ulysses S., 16, 23-24, 47, 98, 174
Greene, Nathanael, 18-20

H

Hahnemann, Samuel, 23, 118, 206-208
Hale, Nathan, 49-50
Hamilton, Alexander, 18, 63-65
Hancock, Winfield Scott, 47, 57-59, 176
Henry, Joseph, 46-47
Heritage and Guardianship, 43-44

I

Isabella I, Queen, 13, 103-105
Iwo Jima, 26, 106, 145-146

J

Jackson, Andrew, 18, 65-67, 73, 75, 189-190
Jefferson Memorial, 139-143
Joan of Arc, 181-182
Johnson, Lyndon Baines, 151, 154-155
Jones, John Paul, 23, 80, 117-118
Juarez, Benito, 94

K

Kennedy, John F., 89, 148-150, 197
Korean War Veterans Memorial, 100-103
Kosciuszko, Thaddeus, 38, 65, 73, 83-85, 139

L

Lafayette, Gilbert de, 37, 65, 73, 75-78, 81
Lincoln Memorial, 47, 72, 110, 119-121, 126
Lincoln Statue, 47-48
Logan, John A., 41, 183-184
Longfellow, Henry Wadsworth, 177-179
Luther, Martin, 194-196

M

Madison, James, 18, 62-63
Marshall, John, 45-46
Mason, George, National Memorial, 18, 57, 137-139
McClellan, George B., 14, 59, 175-176
McPherson, James B., 77, 184
Meade, George Gordon, 40-44
Mellon, Andrew W., Memorial Fountain, 33-34
Motherland, 92-93

N

National Law Enforcement Officers Memorial, 50-53
Navy, U.S., Memorial, 53-56
Navy-Marine Memorial, 151-154
Nuns of the Battlefield, 198-199, 201

P

Peace Monument, 20-21
Pershing, John J., 80-81
Pike, Albert, 31-32
Pulaski, Casimir, 37-38, 84
Pushkin, Alexander, 91-92

Q

Queen Isabella I, 13, 103-105

R

Rawlins, John A., 98-99
Red Cross Monument, 105-107
Red Cross Spirit, 105-107
Rochambeau, Jean de, 65, 73, 75, 77-79
Roosevelt, Franklin Delano, Memorial, 130-136
Roosevelt, Theodore, 79, 86, 130, 154-157, 175, 199

S

Scott, Winfield, 20, 212-213
Second Division Memorial, 82-83, 134
Settlers of the District of Columbia Memorial, 83
Sheridan, Philip H., 199-201
Sherman, William Tecumseh, 23, 47, 77, 85-87
Shevchenko, Taras, 209
Signers of the Declaration of Independence Monument, 108-109

Spirit of Nursing, The, 96-98
Steuben, Friedrich Wilhelm von, 65, 73-74, 124

T

Taft, Robert A., 22
Thomas, George H., 17, 176-177, 200
Titanic Memorial, 94, 211-212
Tomb of the Unknowns, 158-162

U

U.S.S. *Maine* Memorial, 129-130
United States Marine Corps Memorial, 145-146
Unknowns, Tomb of the, 158-162

V

Veterans of Foreign Wars Memorial, 25-27, 106
Vietnam Veterans Memorial, 110-114
Vietnam Women's Memorial, 114-115
Von Steuben, Friedrich Wilhelm, 65, 73-74, 124

W

Washington Monument, 110, 119, 121-122, 126
Washington, George, Lieutenant General, 188-190
Webster, Daniel, 168-170
Witherspoon, John, 186-188
World War I Memorial, 124
World War II Memorial, 124-127